Virtually New for Virtually Nothing

Maximizing Your Resources in Today's Challenging Economic Times

Written by Kim Moeller, M.L.A., C.E.B.S

VIRTUALLY NEW FOR VIRTUALLY NOTHING

International Standard Book Number: 1-4675-9631-2
Cover design and book layout by Liz King
Unless otherwise indicated, Scripture quotations are from:
The Holy Bible, New International Version

Printed in the United State of America

Way back in 2001 and 2002, Kim was one of my five in my discipling group. She was then – and is now ever more so – godly, steady, wise, and unconsciously beautiful: a blessing to her husband, her children, her friends (including me), and her audiences. I commend her to you and her book, *Virtually New for Virtually Nothing.*

Anne Ortlund, *Author/Speaker, Lido Island, California.*

Kim's energy and enthusiasm is contagious! She lights up the room as she shares her passion for making a difference in our world. She both challenges and encourages people to discover their gifts and to use those gifts to reach others.

Betty Southard, *Author, Speaker, CLASSeminar Instructor, Newport Beach, California*

Kim is a woman who lives what she speaks and writes. She's the real deal and inspires women to believe God can use their lives, talents, and resources for His kingdom. She herself is living an ordinary life in an extraordinary way. I appreciate her warmth, insight, and great ideas!

Jennifer DeKlotz, *College Counselor, Irvine, California*

I highly recommend Kim as a very personal and engaging speaker and writer! I heard her speak during a President's Forum and she was very well received by our audience – especially the women! You will be blessed by reading this book, *Virtually New for Virtually Nothing.*

Gonny Gutierrez, *Global Program Director, Alpha-1, Miami, Florida*

Dedication

This book is dedicated to my husband, Carl, and to my four kids: Caroline, James, Claire, and Alexandra. Thank you for giving me the time to work on this project. You know me better than anyone else does. You know my love for bargains and my desire to get the best deal out there. And, you share in my love for the Kingdom and in maximizing our family's resources for Him. Thank you for making this dream of mine possible and for allowing me to share my dream with others.

I love you all dearly.

Kim

Table of Contents

7 Virtually New for Virtually Nothing

Author's Note

It is my hope that after reading this book, you will feel as though you have come away with a new pair of glasses with which to see the world! There are some things that we learn and some things that happen to us, which cause us to never again see the world in the same way. I believe this is a big part of the purpose of our life's journey and something to be excited about embracing!

Our time here on earth is brief and it's crucial that we each realize the powerful role we all play in the overall drama. You were chosen uniquely by God to be a steward of resources for you and your family, and to take a lead role in His play. Does it amaze you to know that the decisions you make today at the grocery store or on your family's furnishings, or vacation can have a profound eternal impact?

"Show me, O Lord, my life's end and the number of my days; let me know how fleeting is my life. You have made my days a mere handbreadth; the span of my years is as nothing before you. Each man's life is but a breath." Psalms 39:4-5

Can you look at each day with all of the purchasing and financial decisions you make, as decisions for eternity? Whether we like it or not, how we manage our resources will have an impact on our future both here and in eternity. God wants to see how wisely we manage His financial resources, whether it is a dollar or a million dollars. Our God wants to be believed for great things and to be glorified through the mighty acts that He performs. We have a one time opportunity to live by faith while on this earth and to see all that He can do through us, with willing and teachable hearts. He allows us to trust Him, to make mistakes, and to pick ourselves back up again and to keep going.

Come journey with me as we discover tips along the way to maximize that with which we have been entrusted, and glorify Him in the process. We truly do have just a limited number of days here on this earth. On the days that are long and difficult, it FEELS like our time here is forever. But it is not. One day, we will stand before God and like you, my deepest desire is that He would say, "*Well done, my good and faithful servant.*" *Matthew 25:21*

He's given us some great tips in His word on why we should live for eternity and how to do it. So go and grab a cup of tea, a highlighter, and pen to mark up this book, and let's put on a radical new pair of glasses and get started!

Kim Moeller
August 16, 2013

One

Maximizing Your Money for Eternity

"I must learn to number my days so I may get a heart of wisdom." Psalms 143:10

Every hot and sticky summer, my family used to respect each others' lines on the vinyl car upholstery and drive up the cool, central coast to my grandparents' little beach house. And, invariably, we would remember to bring the Monopoly game. It would occupy my sisters and beach house friends for hours. We would play sometimes for days, building our real estate holdings and empires.

One windy, cold vacation, we pulled up to the little two room house and realized we had forgotten the Monopoly board! We played the game so often that I knew every single property and the purchase price on the board. So, not to be deterred, my friend and I created our own Monopoly board on a huge, brown paper bag! And, we almost had more fun playing the game as we tried to recreate everything about it that we could remember. We had markers so we colored every property the right color, remembered their selling prices, and even remembered a number of the Chance and Community Chest cards.

Monopoly is an incredible game, very similar to the real game all of us play in life every day. We earn money, we take risks (some of us more than others), we make investments, we lose money, and sometimes we're fortunate and we get a "get out of jail free" card. We land on Community Chest and we land on Chance. And, in the end, someone wins the game and the pieces all go back in the box and the game is over.

However, there is one significant difference for people who are followers of Christ. There will not be a single winner in life's game. Instead, God will look at each one of us and see how well we played the game according to HIS rules. We only have a certain amount of money, a certain amount of time, and He wants to see what you are going to do with what He has entrusted you with here on earth. And when you stand before Him in Heaven, don't you just long to hear – *"Well done, my good and faithful servant?" Matthew 25:21*

God is definitely not into the world's idea of he who dies with the most toys wins. You see, God makes a big deal about money and how we use it and think about it in His word because it matters for each of us forever. This truth is based on the completely opposite principle of collecting things for ourselves. Instead, He gives us everything so He can see how we can wisely use them and give our resources to bless others. Our stewardship has eternal significance. This time on earth is like a dress rehearsal for the real deal in heaven. I really don't want to mess this up, and I'm sure you don't either!

It might amaze you to know that there are over 2350 verses devoted to money in the Bible. There are approximately twice as many verses regarding money compared to verses on both faith and prayer. It has often been said, if you want to see someone's priorities look at their checkbook and their calendar. "It must be important to God as 15% of His word is devoted to the subject of money. "What you do with your resources in this life is your autobiography," [1] Randy Alcorn, *Money, Possessions, and Eternity.*

[1]*Randy Alcorn, Money, Possessions, and Eternity (Carol Stream, IL: Tyndale House Publishers, Inc., 2003), p. 120.*

WISE LIVING WITH A LITTLE OR A LOT

Why I am so passionate about this subject? Every day is precious, a gift from God, and when we embrace that truth we begin to live differently. We do not know how long we will be here on this earth. And, in these challenging economic times, we have all seen how quickly wealth can disappear. As a result, we have a limited opportunity to maximize what we have and a responsibility to be wise, not wasteful, stewards.

Some of you may be reading this book knowing that you do not have a penny to spare in your budget. Or, every penny is needed for some non-fun, essential line item such as electricity, gas, or water. Believe me, I have been there. I remember when I quit my well-paying secular consultant job to stay at home with our first two children. We did not have a penny to spare. Our big treat was a weekly pizza for the family. Many years went by where we scrimped and saved every extra dollar we could. Because of the lessons we learned in those years with young children, we still consider each and every dollar as valuable.

Just before the boom in the housing market, we moved out to California almost a decade ago. We looked at numerous homes, but wanted to be in a particular school district so our choices were limited. As a result, the only house we were able purchase was a home where the wallpaper had been painted over in order to sell the place. The funny thing was this "little" piece of information was not disclosed before the sale. We realized this AFTER the documents were signed!

The house had twenty foot ceilings with wallpaper from the floor to the ceiling. Days and days were spent stripping and stripping the painted wallpaper off of the walls. Our kids were 6, 4, 2, and six months so, it was a little crazy to say the least. We have had to put sweat equity into every house we have ever purchased.

Prior to having kids while living in Chicago, there was another time where we did not have enough money in our budget to fix the reverse gear in my husband's Ford Bronco II. For six months, Carl literally had no reverse gear, and had to park in places where he would be able to leave by driving forward. We had worked as Christian missionaries, I had my bachelor's degree and master's degree and we still did not have enough money for a reverse gear. So, for those of you who can relate, I have been there!

The topic of maximizing our resources during these challenging economic times is pertinent for everyone. We have all been faced with financial challenges over the past couple of years since our nation's recent economic collapse. Some of us have lost jobs, some have lost homes, our savings/college accounts have been decimated, some have taken pay cuts, and businesses seem to be closing around us left and right.

Perhaps you have weathered the economic collapse relatively well and are among the fortunate few who have not been severely affected by our economy. Or, perhaps you fall somewhere in between. Perhaps you have made poor financial decisions in the past (who hasn't?!) or spent your money frivolously when you had a lot of it. No worries. Today is a new day and God can always redeem what we have messed up in our humanness. The key is to keep going and to not quit seeking Him for wisdom. He will bless your efforts and decisions when you want to do what is right to please Him. If any of the above is true for you, this book is also for you. No matter how little or how much money you have today, my goal is to inspire you to maximize all of it for God's kingdom.

Webster's Dictionary defines maximize as "to make the most out of" something. God desires for us to maximize what He has given us. This means if He gives us $100, we are to make the most out of every penny of that $100. When we seek Him for wisdom regarding how to spend our money, our resources will be multiplied. The original $100 can turn out to be worth $1000, when spent and invested wisely. The message of this book has been on my heart for a long time. I believe the principles contained in these pages will deeply encourage you and remind you that in the midst of all of this chaos, our God has not changed. He is still here and He is faithful and He wants to provide for each of us in amazing and creative ways.

We're going to look at some practical ways that you can purchase items that are virtually new for virtually nothing! You will find pragmatic ways for you to stretch the dollar and be amazed at what is available around us for a fraction of the retail price. And, more importantly, we are going to look at how we all have been blessed to be a blessing to others by maximizing and sharing our resources!

Obviously, if God is devoting so much of His word to how we handle money, then we need to make the most of whatever He has given us. You see, I am a maximizer by nature. I'm the kind of person when I find a bargain or a money saving tip, I want to share it with everyone! Out of necessity because of working in the ministry and living in southern California with a high cost of living, I have had to learn how to save dollars, and stretch our budget. Although there were many, many times when I wondered how it would all work out, God has always been faithful to provide in incredible ways.

ALL STAR BLITZ

There is a special story that comes to my mind regarding God's incredible provision. I was a senior in college and had decided that I was going to go on the mission field with a Christian organization called Cru. This was a huge step of faith for me as it meant that I would need to raise my support. I would need to approach individuals and businesses and see who might be interested in sending me a monthly or annual devotion to support my missions work.

Well, God must have known that I needed to have a little extra boost of help from Him as I needed to raise money for lodging, food, a car, clothes etc...Being that I went to school in LA, there were always unique opportunities because of the proximity to Hollywood and Beverly Hills. One day, I saw an ad that a pilot game show was looking for contestants called, "All Star Blitz". It was a bit like Hollywood Squares where you were up against a contestant of the opposite sex and then you had to agree or disagree with the famous stars' answers. Needless to say, I applied and was accepted!

I borrowed a roommate's car and drove to Hollywood with several changes of clothes in tow. They filmed the entire week's shows on a Monday and had everyone in the studio from about 2:00 pm to 11:00 pm straight. All of the contestants sat in an area of the set waiting to see if we would be next to be selected to be on the show. Well, one of the male contestants was fluent in seven languages and brilliant. He kept winning and winning and beating all of the female contestants.

I was, by far, the youngest female contestant on the set. Tony, the contestant coordinator, picked every other woman but me to go up against him. So, now here we were at 10:30 at night with the last remaining segment of Friday's show to be filmed. If the woman on the show won, then I could go home. I prayed that I would not be picked at this point. It was the first day of my quarter at UCLA, and I just wanted to get back to my sorority and pretend this day had never happened.

Well, God had a plan that was quite different than mine. The female contestant lost and because I was the only other female left, I was placed on the show. At this point, the male game show winner had taken his earnings and left the show. I was now up against a young man about five years older than me. We played one round and he won. If he could just win the second round, then I would be finished. I'd take my life time supply of beef jerky and go home. But no! The winner had to win two out of three rounds. I ended up winning my round and we were tied.

I drove back to my sorority, Kappa Kappa Gamma, feeling so

discouraged. Now, this meant not only did I miss a day of classes but I would need to come back the following Monday and finish the show. I couldn't believe it!

The following Monday, my mom drove up to UCLA because she wanted to watch me on the show. I walked out of the sorority house with two changes of clothes. She asked, "Where are all of your outfits you are supposed to bring?'

"Mom," I replied, "You know I am just going to lose and have to go home!"

So, we drove to Hollywood for the second day of taping. I prayed that God would be honored, glorified, through this situation however crazy it seemed to me at the time. I said hello to Tony and to all of the new contestants and I took my place on the stage. And, I began to win and to win, and to win! I beat the young man on Monday's show, and continued to win all the way through Wednesday's show. (Did I mention that on national TV I now had NOTHING to wear?!!!) By Wednesday's show I was combining Monday's jacket with Tuesday's skirt, etc...

My mom was so excited that she said we had to drive an hour south to our family's home to show my dad some of the winnings. I actually walked off the set in a fur coat and carrying two tennis rackets. To make a very long story short, this is how God provided through the game show: enough money to finance my grad school education and purchase a car; a trip to Jamaica that my girlfriends and I went on for college graduation; a trip to Mexico City for a week for two; and a trip to Europe for two that I ended up giving to my parents for their 25th anniversary.

Peter Marshall, the host of this show, and I ended up really connecting during the breaks and having discussions of a spiritual nature. What amazed me was the influence of TV in our culture and how many random people saw this show televised. I was standing in line at UCLA buying some books and a guy yelled to me, "Hey, I just saw you when I got out of the shower!" Apparently, his TV was on and this game show was televised at the time. I don't know what the people who were standing in line were thinking when they heard him!

I share this story with you to show you how God can burst all of our boxes. He will not fit into a box. When He is calling you to do something, He will provide from His unlimited supply of resources. Nine times out of ten, it will be in ways you never expected. He will provide so that He can meet your temporal needs as well as send things on ahead for you for eternity because you trusted Him.

PASS GO AND SEND ON YOUR $200 FOR ETERNITY!

Now, let's get back to the Monopoly game board. There is one big important piece missing from this game. Nowhere on the board is there any mention of heaven or investing in eternity, just like the world in which we live! Billboards advertise what we can buy rather than how to invest in God's eternal kingdom.

God's word tells us,"*Keep your lives free from the love of money and be content with what you have, because God has said, "Never will I leave you: never will I forsake you." Hebrews 13:5*

Luke 16:13, "No servant can serve two masters. Either he will hate the one and love the other, or he will be devoted to the one and despise the other. You cannot serve both God and Money."

In the big scheme of things, He will not care if we purchased all three light blue properties or had to mortgage some of them to pay the bills. He will care about our hearts and whether we realized that everything comes from Him and we held things loosely.

If we know where we are headed, if we have the big picture in mind and the overall target before us, it becomes much simpler to navigate our course. God tells us that He has set eternity in our hearts. Some choose to follow Him and others do not. This life is a test. A very short, one page test, that will help to determine our destiny.

That sounds awfully serious; surely it could not be so simple. And yet, it is profoundly elementary. God gives us things, money, possessions to manage for Him during our brief time on earth. He watches to see how we manage them. Where are our hearts? Are we possessive? Do we falsely think that everything is ours and we can choose to do what we want without consequences? Or, do we realize we are being tested to see what is really at the core of our motives? When we understand that everything comes from Him and is owned by Him, then our financial decisions need to be prayed over and our resources held with open hands so He can lead and direct us.

God is watching. The Bible tells us that riches are fleeting. *"Whoever trusts in his riches will fall, but the righteous will thrive like a green leaf." Proverbs 11:28*

He allows us to make our own choices and to live with the consequences both good and bad. He does not want puppets here on earth or in heaven. He wants those people who truly want to live all out for Him with their time, talents, and treasures.

"HAVING IT ALL" TO HAVING ABSOLUTELY NOTHING

In the March 23, 2009 edition of Sports Illustrated there was an article entitled, "How (and why) Athletes Go Broke." The article went on to say that it didn't matter how much money the athletes brought in on their contracts. The multiple ways they blow their money are very similar to one another. The article stated, "Professional athletes' salaries have risen steadily in the last three decades. But by the time NFL players have been retired two years, 78% of them either have gone bankrupt or are under financial stress because of joblessness or divorce." Remember, this quote means that millions of dollars are virtually gone! One day the money is in their bank accounts and then gone the next.

Most of us individuals will not be entrusted with the wealth in our lifetimes as the professional athletes. All of us, however, will be judged on what little or large amount of money we have and what we did with it. And to a certain degree, we are all faced with the same types of temptations regarding our money as the athletes are: who to trust, mixing family and business, strains on the marriage because of finances, and unmet financial expectations. If those who seem to have unlimited amounts of money can end up bankrupt, perhaps we can keep in mind what not to do and learn from their mistakes.

If we are prudent with a little, imagine what God can do with our resources. God cares about each and every dollar we spend. When we devote our resources to Him, we are blessed. *"Blessed are all who fear the Lord, who walk in His ways. You will eat the fruit of your labor; blessings and prosperity will be yours." Psalm 128: 1-2*

If we live according to our hearts and our emotions, rather than God's principles, there is no doubt we will end up exactly as the athletes mentioned above. The Bible tells us that *"The heart is deceitful above all things and beyond cure. Who can understand it?" Jeremiah 17:9.* When left to our own devices, we will be sorely disappointed. However, when we turn to Him for wisdom He both protects us and provides for us.

HE'S GOT THE WHOLE WORLD IN HIS HANDS

It does not make sense in the world's eyes to fear the Lord. But when we realize who holds the key to everything, it makes complete sense to fear Him, obtain wisdom, and to live according to His ways rather than the ways of the world.

This book is going to challenge you to dream big, to realize how big the God is whom we serve, and to give you a new way of viewing your finances. You will be encouraged and hopeful as you find a new way of looking at spending your money wisely, finding bargains, and maximizing your money in multiple areas of life. You will be challenged to be a generous giver of your resources so that you begin to live for eternity in the here and now.

Alright, let's get started. Let's begin to look at the following topics that we're going to cover with eternity in mind: groceries, furniture, home remodeling to mention a few. This way when the dress rehearsal Monopoly game is over, we will all be winner's in God's eyes for eternity.

ETERNITY CHECKPOINTS

- Ask yourself, "Are my financial decisions impacted by the truth of eternity?"
- What do you (and your spouse, if applicable) believe about the fact that all of your resources were given to you by God?
- Do you hold things loosely?
- Are you a generous giver? When is the last time you gave to God's work, the poor, a homeless person?
- Begin to examine how much of your family's budget is allocated to giving.

ETERNITY ACTION STEP

- Find someone you can bless anonymously this week by giving them money they might need or a resource that you already own.

"He has made everything beautiful in its time. He has also set eternity in the hearts of men; yet they cannot fathom what God has done from beginning to end." Ecclesiastes 3:11

Two

Designer Furniture for Your Budget

"Home is where one starts from." T.S. Elliot

We live in an area of southern California where countless people had boatloads of money during the real estate boom. The money was flowing. People were employed and had more work than they could handle: contractors, painters, gardeners, mortgage brokers, real estate agents just to name a few of the professions. Money was flowing into home remodels, the purchase and sale of new real estate because it seemed like a wise and secure investment. It reminded me a lot of the gold rush...tons of money one day and then it all but disappeared by the next day when the boom ended.

Some people grew very accustomed to very high salaries, furniture trucks were often making deliveries in our neighborhood, and so it was extremely shocking when the huge salaries disappeared. And, I must say that the trucks are not seen very often around here anymore. I've often wondered if people have regretted spending such large sums of money on brand new sets of furniture when now that money is needed for groceries and their mortgage payments.

Since my husband and I have worked in the secular world, and many years in ministry, we have had to live quite frugally all along out of necessity. My husband, Carl, has worked for the bulk of his career in the non-profit sector. As a result, we have raised our four children here for almost the past decade on one salary. It has been quite challenging based on the high price of housing in this area.

Prior to having children, many years of my career were spent in the corporate consulting world, while my husband was a seminary student working part-time. I worked part-time up until our second child was born and have basically been a stay-at-home mom ever since. As a result, I have had to learn to be creative regarding how to best manage our resources and to stretch the dollar. The problem is that I have always had champagne tastes often with a much smaller budget. I'm sure you can relate!

We are going to look at the many components that women need to consider when running a household. Some are weekly expenditures such as groceries, and some are more lifetime purchases such as furniture. Regardless of the category of expenses, there are creative ways that you can find what you like or need for a much better price than retail. Let's begin by looking at furniture ideas for your home and how you can furnish your home in the style and design you love for much less than the stores would love to have you think you can.

As a result of a lot of bargain hunting, most of the furnishings in my home today are mostly the Ethan Allen furniture brand or Pottery Barn. However, of all of the furnishings only a small Ethan Allen table and a bed canopy were purchased brand new. Everything else was purchased on eBay, Craig's List, at a local consignment store, or at a garage sale.

Put on your new glasses and allow me to share some of my secrets and favorite finds with you; give you some pros and cons about eBay, Craig's List, and consignment stores; and change the way you ever look at furniture again!

FURNITURE FACTS

Did you know that brand new furniture depreciates the MOMENT you buy it, very similar to an automobile? Have you ever gotten a scratch on a brand new piece of furniture and just felt sick about it? I've found that I feel less sick WHEN (not if) it happens if:

1. I did not purchase it brand new.
2. It already had some little scratch or ding on it that brought the price down by around 75%.

Do you have kids? Do you have pets? Do you have a spouse? Chances are 99% likely that one of them will put the next scratch on your furniture. The potential savings in buying used furniture is huge!! The benefits far outweigh the stress in locating the items and getting them to your home without the furniture store taking care of it for you.

So how do we get started?

First of all, begin collecting photos of the styles of furniture you like. Find a plastic bin where you can store your magazine photos. (You don't need to keep the entire magazine either. Just tear out the photos you like, and make sure you keep the name and date of the magazine issue.) Try to figure out what style and time period of furniture is best suited for you. You may have grown up with parents who loved a certain decorating style. Maybe you have a different sense of style?!

Think of the places you've been, the homes you've visited and loved. What types of furniture are you most at home with? What type of furniture creates the ambiance that you want to convey in your home? Perhaps you enjoy the Asian influence, or maybe modern, French country, or shabby chic is for you? Or maybe there is a certain type of store that just shouts out your name like Pottery Barn, or Crate and Barrel, or the catalog, Ballard Designs.

It's really helpful when you find the catalogs with the various furniture prices listed in them, that you hold onto these. I have narrowed my decorating style down to a blend of French Country and Swedish Country. The furniture pieces I gravitate toward have the old world European feel. I absolutely love the two collections that Ethan Allen carries of these furniture pieces. The Swedish Collection has been discontinued; however, I still have an Ethan Allen catalog that shows me the dimensions and original prices of these pieces. The catalog gives me ideas when I see a piece and I wonder, "Does this look Swedish? Would it go with my other pieces?"

The catalogs are extremely helpful for when I find an item on eBay and I need to know how high I am willing to bid for the item.

COUNTRY SWEDISH CASE STUDY

I once found an Ethan Allen Swedish Country king-sized bed frame at a consignment store. The frame alone was close to $1200 new. I wasn't quite ready to make the purchase with my budget. So, I waited a month or so. (Normally, you do not have the luxury to do this when it is a good deal.) I went back to the consignment store and the bed frame was still there. They were asking $800 for it. I asked them how low they were willing to go with it. They said they would sell it to me for $600, half of the original price, in absolutely perfect condition.

Now, the best part of the story is a couple of months later I was searching the "Ethan Allen" furniture section of eBay. I was narrowing down the search under the category of Swedish Country. Sure enough, there was the exact bedroom furniture to match my king bed frame that I had bought. It included a queen bed frame.

I emailed her and asked if she would be willing to sell just the two nightstands, the upholstered chair and ottoman, and the armoire. She said yes, and I ended up being the only one who bid on this auction. Her prices were a third of the original price of Ethan Allen's prices. Now, I had to factor in shipping because she was located in Kansas and I lived in Southern California. Before I placed my bid, I had contacted a freight company that would come to her house and crate the furniture and truck it to me. Because I had the catalog, I knew the furniture dimensions and I guesstimated the weight.

In the end, the shipping and auction price turned out to be about half of the original Ethan Allen retail price. I now have a bedroom set that matches perfectly, and a great story to tell!

There are a variety of ways you can go about purchasing your furniture. I have identified the top four methods: eBay, Craig's List, furniture consignment stores, and garage sales. Under each title you will find the pros and cons that you will want to keep in mind before making your purchase.

With any of these options, remember to work within your budget first. Even if you find a $2000 bed that is being sold for $400 but your budget only supports $200 at that time, resist and say no! Always remember to work within the means God has given you. He will provide in His timing. There will be a lot less stress in your marriage too when you both agree to spend within your means and not a penny more.

EBAY PROS AND CONS

Pros:

- There is a wide variety of merchandise available because it is grouped by category and not location. You can search on the item across eBay as a whole, rather than by city like on Craig's List.
- It is an auction format. You can sometimes end up with an amazing price, provided you are not outbid.
- You can often buy items through PayPal, so you know that your purchase is guaranteed, should you not receive it.

Cons:

- Starting prices tend to be higher than on Craig's List or at a consignment store.
- Sometimes you may find something you love, but get outbid in an auction. You can avert this by buying something at the "buy it now" price, although this is not always available.
- It's often not local so you are not able to go and see the item firsthand prior to purchasing it.

Your location will determine what types of a selection you will have available on the resale market. If you live near a big city such as New York City, Chicago, or Los Angeles, you will be more likely to have more options. Most of my furniture has been purchased via Craig's List in my surrounding areas. But that is not to say that it is not possible to still find a great deal in a far away city and to have it delivered to you.

Let me give you some tips that have really helped me in my furniture searches on Craig's List.

USING CRAIG'S LIST EFFECTIVELY

Type www.craigslist.com into your browser.

Next, begin by identifying the geographical area that you would like to search. You will see the various available locations on the right side of the screen. I live in Orange County, California. There happens to be a button just for Orange County. (One of the great things about living in this area is that people get rid of perfectly nice things, ALL the time. In other areas such as Salt Lake City where the average income is not quite as high, and people tend to have a lot of children, you might not find quite the selection nor quality after it's been loved on for a long time!)

Nevertheless, I begin by searching under "furniture" in Orange County. You will find the furniture heading in the middle of your screen. I also usually end up searching San Diego, Los Angeles, and sometimes the Inland Empire. For some reason, I have had the most success in the San Diego area. If you don't see the area listed on the main screen that you are looking for, click on your state's name to the far right and you will see some additional choices.

After I have clicked on furniture, I specify the furniture brand that I would like to find. For example, I might type in "Pottery Barn". Then, the computer will pull up for me all of the listings from the most current to the oldest listing in the last 30 days. I work from the top of the screen down as the top are the most recent, and I have the most likely chance of getting them before they are sold to someone else.

I might want to narrow my search because I am looking specifically for a full bed from the Pottery Barn. So, I could type in "Pottery Barn full bed". It will pull up any listings in Orange County that meet that criterion. You will also notice that it will specify whether or not a picture is included next to the posting on the first "furniture" screen. I usually do not waste my time if there is no picture unless it seems like an incredible deal, Then, I will email the seller for a photo.

Most listings where the seller is serious about selling their item, will have photos of the furniture. You can then sit at your desk and shop! You can decide, "Yes, that looks like what I am looking for...or no, I can tell that piece is not in good condition." Once I find the item I am looking for, I email the seller. Sometimes, a phone number is listed but usually it is just a reply to their ad. If the seller is requesting to be contacted by phone, by all means contact him by phone. It's usually your fastest way of getting to the seller.

If the seller is handling everything through email, then all you do to reply is click on the reply to sender. You will notice it does not show the seller's home email. (This is good to keep in mind when you desire to sell some item on Craig's List.) It will, however, show the seller's home email address when they respond to your email inquiry.

So, I email the seller. My email usually looks something like this:

"Hi,

I am interested in your full size Pottery Barn bed frame. Can you please tell me on a scale of 1-10 what condition it is in, with 10 being the best? Can you please tell me why you are selling it? I live in ______________, so I am local and could come over at your earliest convenience to look at it.

Thank you!
Kim"

Now, if it is a hot item with an amazing price, then you will want to put in your phone number with your response. "Please call me as soon as possible as I would love to purchase your item, or have a look at it."

I have bought a number of things sight unseen. My husband once picked up an Ethan Allen leather couch for me. The seller had paid $6200 for it, and we purchased it for $1100. The woman was selling it because her son had allergies and she couldn't vacuum underneath it. Otherwise, it was in perfect condition. I could tell by her detailed email answering my questions that it was in fabulous shape. And, I knew if I didn't send my husband to go and buy it that it would be gone.

So, he rented a U-Haul on his way home from work, and drove to Riverside about an hour away to buy it. It's a good thing he did, because apparently the lady had ten other people interested in the couch. They were even willing to pay more than I did. She kept her word and sold the couch to me. I emailed her to thank her and tell her how much I loved the couch when my husband delivered it. I felt badly for her because I think she had seller's remorse in having to even get rid of such a fine piece of furniture.

She had actually listed the sofa on Craig's List in the Inland Empire section almost a month prior. I had seen it and had emailed her but thought that the dimensions were too big for my space. So, then she had discounted the price and it still wasn't selling. She decided to list her ad in the Los Angeles section of Craig's List. As soon as she did that she had a buying frenzy on her hands. There is a hot market for Ethan Allen in Los Angeles, and more buying power than the Inland Empire usually has.

Fortunately, because I was one of the first to respond when she listed her ad in the LA section, she chose to sell me the couch. A neighbor, Vicki, who is also an avid Craig's List buyer/seller, actually notified me when she saw it posted in LA. And now, we enjoy the beautiful chocolate brown leather couch in our bonus room every night. I figure the $75 we had to spend on the U-Haul, was well worth getting a $6200 couch for $5000 less!

PROS/CONS OF CRAIG'S LIST

Pros:

- The item can usually be located locally, when you are searching in surrounding areas.
- The prices are cheaper than a consignment store where the seller is having to pay a commission.
- There is no auction involved. So, you know that the price listed is the price the seller is asking. Most times, the seller will negotiate with you and accept a discounted price.
- You can search by the brand name of the item and usually see photos, so it saves you time from driving around to various garage sales or consignment stores.

Cons:

- You need to have the time in your schedule to respond quickly, otherwise the item will be sold.
- The item could have a scratch on it that you are not aware

of in the posting. This is why it is important to ask discerning questions in your email.

You always need to be careful of who is selling the item, or who is buying from you. If I am buying something by myself, I will usually meet the individual at a parking lot by a store location rather than going to the individual's residence. When in doubt, do not do business with anyone you do not trust. (I once met a woman having a type of garage sale on Craig's List. She said that she was only responding to women who answered her ads. That was her prerogative!)

It takes a bit more time to sometimes wait for the right item to be posted. Sometimes, it involves checking the computer quite often so you do no miss the good deals. And always remember that EVERYTHING is negotiable. Most times, the seller wants to get rid of the item and they are willing to negotiate with you.

I determine how much I will offer by a variety of criterion. First, I usually have a good idea of how much the item is worth and how the seller's price compares. Second, I will pay more if they are willing to deliver it to me or meet me half way somewhere to save me the gas and time. Third, if they are getting a lot of calls on the item I know I need to act quickly and offer pretty close to the asking price or I will lose the item. When I make my offer, I always offer lower than I am really willing to pay. It gives the seller a chance to arrive at the final price on his own and then he feels like he got what he wanted for the item.

Remember to always be a person of your word. If you say you are going to go and look at an item, do it. Do not keep the person waiting. I will usually give them a half hour window of time. I will say, "I will be there between 5:00 – 5:30. Can I trust that you will hold the item for me until then and not sell it to someone else?" I had one experience where I arrived right before the armoire was sold right out from under me. I learned from that experience to clarify up front the terms.

You need to have cash to pay for the item. Or, you can pay for the item with PayPal.

PAYPAL CASE STUDY

Allow me to tell you my fun experience with PayPal. I had just dropped my kids off one morning and my friend, Vicki, mentioned to me that she had just seen an incredible Craig's Listing of Ethan Allen furniture on Coronado Island in San Diego. Coronado Island is about an hour and fifteen minutes' drive from my home. I went on the listing and a young man was selling his deceased grandmother's furniture in her Coronado penthouse. He had taken at least fifteen pictures from her beach condo showing an EA dining room set, sofa set, dressers, lamps, pictures, rugs, and accessories. The prices were 75% less than retail Ethan Allen prices!

People on Craig's List went wild and started emailing him like crazy. He had posted his phone number, so I called him. I told him that I would be interested in the lamps, the Swedish round table, the coffee table, the EA painted dresser and the shell vase. Well, he was not prepared for the response that he received from tons of people. He realized that he had listed everything far too low. So he changed the listing, apologized to me and now was asking prices that were 65% less than retail.

They were still amazing deals. Everything was beachy white and brand new. The grandmother lived on the east coast and had only stayed in this condo a handful of nights. Since so many people wanted these items, he was taking deposits on PayPal. PayPal is a credit card system where you can enter the person's email where the payment is going, and pay by credit card. It felt a little iffy to be putting down a deposit on things I had not yet seen in person, but I left deposits on all of the items. (I knew that I could cancel the payments if the man skipped out on the deal.)

My next dilemma was to figure out how to get all of these

items into my Honda Odyssey mini van, an amazing storage vehicle that once fit my entire EA kitchen dining set. We had it all arranged for my husband to pick up the items. And, at the last minute he had to go out of town and I was the only one who could get the items.

I met the seller in the parking lot and I then followed him to an exclusive penthouse high rise on Coronado, complete with a bellman and everything. There were other individuals there picking up their items as well. I prayed that someone could help me load all of this furniture into my van! Sure enough, a nice couple was there and the husband and the seller loaded everything into my van. And, everything fit perfectly!

Now, my dilemma was how to get the furniture out of my van because a lot of it was too heavy for me to lift. Sure enough when I got home there were two guys working on my air conditioning unit. I asked them if I could pay them to unload my van for $50 and they were glad to help out.

There is one more part of this story. The grandmother had a beautiful brand new, never been used, EA white Swedish Country dining room set. At 65% of the retail price, it was still too high for my budget. I told the seller how much I liked the set and to call me if he wasn't able to sell it. He had a deadline where he had to have all of the furniture out of the condo because it was being sold. A couple of days later he emailed me to say that he was willing to sell it to me for $800. The retail price new is $ 3000. It was a great price but with my recent purchases, I had very little left in the budget. I told him I could pay $650 and no more.

He ended up selling it to me and my sweet husband drove to Coronado when he returned from his business trip and fit the entire set into our mini van! Now aren't these stories a lot more fun than just walking into a retail store and paying full price? I barely get excited when I see furniture sales advertised because I know that their bottom line prices are still going to be SO much higher than I pay on Craig's List.

I used to go into the Ethan Allen showroom and almost feel rather depressed. I would love their displays and then look at the prices and think there was no way in this world, I could afford their furniture. Now, I look around my home and almost 75% of it is Ethan Allen all purchased at 50 – 90% of the retail cost.

SELLING FURNITURE YOURSELF

Now, another fun thing to keep in mind is that you can be selling the furniture you do not want anymore from your own home. You can bring it to a consignment store. They will make an agreement with you to sell it for a certain price. You will receive a percentage of the sale, usually somewhere between 40-60% of the price. If the item is in the store for a while, they will often reduce the original price quoted to you. Some consignment stores will pick up the furniture items for you, others you need to deliver the furniture yourself.

Usually when the consignment store is unable to sell your item, they will offer you the option to have it donated. Or, you can come and pick it up from them. My theory is that if it didn't sell in the consignment store, it's probably best to just donate the item. Bless someone else less fortunate and call it a day! You wanted to get rid of the item in the first place, so please do not bring it back home!

CONSIGNMENT STORE PROS AND CONS

Pros:

- You can walk into the store to see the actual item.
- A lot of times, the consignment store will take less for the item, usually up to 20% if it has been on the floor for a while.
- My local consignment store has a test drive policy. I can buy the item and they charge it to my credit card. I can take the

item home and try it out for 24 hours. If I do not contact them prior to the 24 hour period being up, the item is mine. Should I decide that I do not like it, I can return it and get all of my money back.

Cons:

- You cannot search on the internet for the item you are looking for. (I once knew a consignment store that had their items posted online. But, they went out of business, and they also had a hard time keeping their listings current.) So, you need to drive to the store and ask the store salespeople if they have the brand or style you are looking for.
- Prices tend to be higher than on Craig's List, because they are having to pay a commission to the seller.
- You usually need to arrange transportation of the item to your home.

RESELLING FURNITURE ON THE INTERNET CASE STUDY

Sometimes when you get a really good deal on Craig's List or eBay, you can turn around a sell the item and even make a profit.

One time, I purchased a brand new, in the box Pottery Barn full sized headboard for my daughter. When I got it home, I decided I really needed the white finish rather than the honey maple color. I had gotten such a good price on the item, I listed it for higher than I had purchased the item for. I sold it the first day that I posted the ad on Craig's List. The young mom who was buying it for her daughter's room was thrilled because it was so much less than she would have paid retail.

Another time, I had purchased a denim sectional through the classified ads. The owners had taken immaculate care of the sectional. They sold it to me for $300. We loved this couch and all six of us in my family could sit comfortably on it. We moved the couch between three houses over the period of six years. Finally, we came to the point where we wanted a leather sectional for durability and something to have for the long term. I turned around and sold the sectional for $450, six years later! Now, had I purchased the sectional new I probably would have paid over $2000 for it, and my asset would have just depreciated the moment I walked out of the furniture store.

Walk around your house and think strategically. What do I really need to keep? Is my house cluttered, do I need to get rid of some of the items? Am I just holding onto things because I am sentimental?

I heard the story of one gal who really wanted to get involved with Acres of Love, an AIDS orphan ministry in South Africa, and she lived in southern California. She walked around her house and thought what can I sell in order to help the little orphans? And, she did. She sold quite a number of items to help her financially bless that ministry.

Remember, we are just stewards of what we have been given. I try to hold everything loosely because it is really not mine. It has been given to me on loan.

GARAGE SALES

Garage sales are another way to obtain furniture cheaply! I once met a British man standing on his driveway selling things from his American home. He couldn't believe that we had such events as garage sales and was a bit embarrassed! Well, for Americans, it is a great way to clean out the garage. As they say, "One man's junk is another man's treasure."

PROS AND CONS OF GARAGES SALES

Pros:

- People usually just want to get rid of their furniture and do not want to hassle with taking it to a consignment store, etc.... They are often willing to take a lot less for it.
- Garage sale prices are usually the cheapest when you compare to consignment stores, eBay, and Craig's List. It's a perfect time to haggle over the price. That's what you do at a garage sale!
- You can drive home with the piece of furniture, as long as it fits in your vehicle!
- You are able to see the item versus looking at it on the computer.
- Community wide garage sales are great because you can drive around and look at people's driveways all in one neighborhood, without even leaving your car!

Cons:

- You usually have to arrive very early, about ten minutes before the advertised time, such as 6:45 am.
- You don't really know what will be for sale. Sometimes you hit it right and other times it's a bust.
- There is a no return policy!
- You can sometimes come home with too much stuff because it was SO cheap and then your garage becomes cluttered!

FURNITURE FOR FREE

Did you know there is even a section on Craig's List where people are donating items for free? You can find all kinds of furniture that people want to get rid of that very day. So, once again you have to be fast!

I have a fun story to share with you regarding an item I got for free. I love antique Swedish furniture. The Ethan Allen Swedish Country collection is great, but if I can get the real deal straight from Sweden, I will take that hands down. The clincher is that the real antiques from Sweden are very pricey. But with antiques, they retain their value. So, you can pay a pretty steep price up front but it will hold its value over time.

One day, I had the idea to just search under Swedish Country in the furniture section of Craig's List. Lo and behold, there was a posting for a Swedish dining room hutch made in the 1800's. It turned out that a wonderful woman was redecorating her home into the craftsmen style of furniture. She had this Swedish hutch as well as a bookcase cabinet. Both items had been brought over from Sweden. They were beautiful, a little distressed for being over 100 years old, but in wonderful condition.

I happen to be half Swedish and spent my junior year in college abroad at the University of Lund, in Sweden. I speak Swedish and I think this woman loved that about me. She decided to "loan" me these two pieces of furniture. Her children did not like this style, and she did not want to have to pay for storage. So, needless to say, these furniture pieces are now "in storage" in my home. The hutch alone is valued at over $10,000.

I share this story with you because you just never know what will happen when you are creative with your resources. God is a very creative God and provider. Trust Him to meet your needs. Don't ever think that you need to go into debt to meet your own needs. Live with what He has given you, entrust it to Him, and He will multiply it.

FURNISHING A LAKE HOUSE FOR CHEAP - CASE STUDY

Here is another way to think out of the box regarding furniture. I found some darling toile Williams and Sonoma chair pads on Craig's List. The woman, Marianne, was selling all five for $40. They were over $100 when purchased new. She lives right in the community next to mine, and we met because of her ad on Craig's List.

As I was buying the chair pads, we got into a conversation about how much we loved Craig's List. She told me about all of her deals and how she was currently decorating her home in Coto de Caza with all of her Craig's List antique finds. I told her about some of my favorite deals. She said, "You won't believe this but we own a lake house in Traverse City, Michigan that is approximately 2600 square feet. I told my husband that if he would let me remodel the house, I would furnish the entire house with Craig's List."

"So, for the past six months I have been buying nautical, blue and white colored furniture in the southern California area for this home. Once I found everything I was looking for, and the brands were mainly Pottery Barn and Crate and Barrel, my husband loaded up a U-Haul and drove it to Michigan. We furnished the entire house beautifully for $6000.00"

I love this story because I love what it represents. Marianne discovered that with a little bit more creativity, thinking out of the box, and effort, she was able to obtain and achieve what she wanted for a fraction of the cost.

Find the style you love, be patient and go on the bargain hunting quest! There are so many fun opportunities waiting for you out there. I absolutely love my Ethan Allen French Country kitchen table. It came with six white, wheatback chairs. However, I needed a chair and two barstools that match for my kitchen desk and countertop. Sure enough, I found the exact same Ethan

Allen chair in a honey wheat color. A woman was selling just a single chair, exactly what I needed.

This woman was actually now working at the Ethan Allen store in San Diego. She couldn't believe the response she was getting on Craig's List for the Ethan Allen items she was selling. She said to me, "Here my entire home is furnished in Ethan Allen. I can't believe it! Now I am working there and can get a discount. But I really can't believe the kinds of deals that are out there for Ethan Allen on Craig's List!"

I contrast this with a woman in Real Simple, March 2009, and she was asked her favorite purchase? She named a living room set of furniture for $1800. She loves it and purchased it on a zero interest plan and stated how excited she was that she hadn't even begun paying for it yet. This does not sound fun to me. It makes me sad that for $1800 all she got was a little living room set, when this other woman furnished her entire house for $6000. And, just when the "new" living room set will become feeling old or have gotten dirty at 18 months, that is when her payments will begin. No fun!

About a month later, I found someone else on Craig's List in a different area of San Diego who was selling two wheatback barstools. These were also exactly what I needed. He sold them to me for $30 each. They retail for $ 179.00 each. They match the desk chair and are a slight variation of the exact same wood stain color. The table and six chairs, two barstools, and desk chair would have cost over $3000 new. Instead, I paid $650. Quite a significant savings!

My friends tell me how lucky I am all the time and how I am able to find the bargains others can't find. I tell them that it is not true and anyone can locate the bargains. Prayer is first.

"I pray that you would provide what we need. Help me to be a wise steward. Stretch our resources. Open my eyes to see what I might not otherwise see." I firmly believe that God is the one who has given us our resources and He is the one who helps us maximize them. And, when our money goes to non-fun things like car repairs I say, "Ok, Lord, this is your money. If this is how you want to spend it, then that's ok with me!" Amen

ETERNITY CHECKPOINTS

So, in order to have fun with furniture in your life remember these things:

- Determine your style and stick to it! Don't be afraid to get rid of things and don't purchase the item unless it's right for you, even if it is an amazing bargain!
- Keep your catalogs so you have the prices and size of furniture for items you might be looking for.
- Look on Craig's List, eBay, your local consignment store, and garage sales.

Follow the old German proverb, "Choose what you love. Love what you choose."

And remember, furniture does not go with us to heaven!

ETERNITY ACTION STEPS

1. Determine how much of your household budget you would like to budget for furniture in the next year's time.

   $_____________________________.

2. Look around your house and see items that you no longer love and someone else might enjoy. List those items.

   a.

   b.

   c.

   d.

3. Sell those items on one of the online resources or have a garage sale.

   $ _______________total dollars earned.

4. Begin looking for your new furniture items while using your new furniture fund.

   Furniture wish list:

   Item:____________, furniture maker:___________, desired price $___________.

   Item:____________, furniture maker:___________, desired price $___________.

   Item:____________, furniture maker:___________, desired price $___________.

5. Share your bargains with others and write about deals in your area on your blog!

"Do not store up for yourselves treasures on earth, where moth and rust destroy and where thieves break in and steal. But store up for yourselves, treasures in heaven, where moth and rust do not destroy, and where thieves do not break in and steal. For where your treasure is, there your heart will be also." Matthew 6:20

Three

Food for the Frugally Minded

"Part of the secret of success in life is to eat what you like and let the food fight it out inside." Mark Twain

One of the big areas of my family budget is the area of food and groceries. There's no way around it. We have to eat to live. What boggles my mind is how so much time is spent working to pay for food, planning the menus, cutting out coupons, eating more than we want to eat, paying for a gym membership to lose the weight from the food we ate, and starting the cycle all over again!

Several years ago, my four kids ranged from ages 10 to 16, three girls and one boy. The boy is second, 14 years old. One of my children is a swimmer who has six practices a week for two hours each time. You can believe that she is hungry when she gets home. My son is a soccer player with multiple practices a week as well. And my other two girls dance and come home just as hungry. But if you're like me, I'd really rather be buying something "fun" than food! So, I have had to learn how to be creative in this area as well and stretch my dollars as far as they can go.

COUPON CUTTING FOR GROCERIES

I know, you see the words "coupon cutting" and you think, "Nooooooo! I don't have the time nor energy to cut coupons." If you were motivated to do something else with the money you would save from the coupons, would it be worth the inconvenience?

Right now at the time of the publication of this book, double coupons are no longer available at the large grocery chains. I can tell you when they were available, the savings was truly unbelievable. It was not uncommon for me to look at my receipt and see that I had saved $100 and only spent $60. I am hoping that the stores will realize the loyalty of us double coupon shoppers and reinstate them in the future. But in the meantime, let's look at how coupons work and how they can still save us big dollars.

Most grocery stores including a general type of store such as Target accept coupons for their face value. This means that if your coupon is worth $1.00, when you buy the exact item pictured on the coupon, you will get $1.00 taken off of your bill. Learn to separate the food items from the beauty products sold at a grocery store. Price compare and determine which store has the lowest grocery prices and which store has the lowest beauty product prices.

Every major grocery store sends out a colored newspaper flyer once a week. Most of the stores advertise their sales on Sunday through Tuesday. Therefore, it's helpful if you try to shop on these days. The other days of the week will have specials available, but usually the best savings are on these three days. Take a minute to look through the newspaper flyer and cut out any coupons. Be aware of what is for sale in the store(s) that you frequent.

It's helpful if you begin to take note of the rock bottom prices of certain items, for example, such as chicken, ground beef, and fish. When you see that chicken is $1.79 a pound, that's the time to go and stock up. You might want to buy 20 pounds, provided you have freezer space to store it. Most of the time, meat products are not advertised with manufacturer's coupons. Therefore, it's great to pay attention to the newspaper flyers for the best prices.

Stores often rotate their sales every six weeks. So, if you stock up on paper towels, for example, six weeks later they will most likely go on sale again. Of course, you do need to have the storage space for these items.

MAKING YOUR SHOPPING LIST

Look through the flyer and see what is on sale across the board. Use the flyer to plan your menus rather than the other way around. When I was first married, I did not understand this concept. So, I would instead make my menus based on recipes of my mom's. I would come home feeling very overwhelmed with how much I had spent at the grocery store.

PROS AND CONS OF YOUR TYPICAL GROCERY STORE:

ros:

- They usually accept Manufacturer's Coupons.
- They offer some kind of a sale on Sunday – Tuesday in most cases.
- One stop shop where you can get most of your groceries.
- They will usually still bring your groceries out to your car and load them for you.
- They often offer a special "club card" to encourage shopping loyalty at that store.

Cons:

- They can be really pricey on non-grocery items such as pet food, office supplies, and even beauty supplies.
- They will try to creatively advertise items that are not as well priced to get you to buy them.
- You need to remember to give them your club card, or you will not receive the discount.
- You often have to walk to the back of the store to get the basic essentials such as milk, butter, and eggs, so that you will pass by the other items and be tempted to buy them.

You will need to have a Sunday paper in order to find the bulk of your coupons. Sometimes, it's helpful to even purchase an extra Sunday paper at a nearby gas station. The cost of the extra paper is quickly absorbed by all of the coupon savings. You will need to check with your local grocery store to see if they allow two of the same coupons on two identical items.

ORGANIZING YOUR COUPONS

How do you keep coupons organized? It's helpful to purchase a little 5 x 7 inch size coupon organizer. They carry these at grocery stores in the office aisle as well as places like Staples or Target. Take a few minutes to fill out the little tabs that identify the categories. I like to organize the coupons from the front of the organizer to the back according to the aisles of my most frequented grocery store. I leave the first slot open for the coupons once I have found the items in the store.

Did I remind you to NOT bring little kids when you are coupon grocery shopping? It is too stressful and too hard to focus. When my kids were really little, I would sneak out of the house at 6:00 am before my husband left for work and power grocery shop, without little ones!

You can approach coupons in one of two ways. You can cut out what you need for that week ahead and throw away the rest that you know you will not use. Or, you can use the coupons on the items that are priced lowest and save the remaining coupons. Sometimes, those coupon items will come on sale over the next few weeks before the coupon expires. I tend to clip the coupons that I need for the upcoming week, that correlate with rock bottom prices. I do not usually store and then go back through week old coupons.

Over time, I learned the secrets of coupons and planning my meals from what was advertised first or what I had previously stocked up on in my freezer. I was also taught to keep very little to no cash on me in my wallet. Why? Cash is too easy to spend. It's too easy to go through a drive through or to spend it in a store or a restaurant. Then, you do not know where it has gone, it just disappears.

CREDIT CARDS AND FREQUENT BUYER PROGRAMS

I pay with my Visa card 99% of the time. This way, we can keep track of it on Quicken. We also get free airline miles with every dollar we charge on our credit card. We pay off the credit card every month so we are not incurring any interest charges. We do try to put all of our purchases on the card so that we can obtain free miles.

Most grocery stores have their own frequent buyer programs. These are a necessity as they automatically lower your bill when you purchase the participating items. It's simple to join, you just need to fill out a form and they will give you a card or key card to go on your key ring. I find it's easiest to just put them all on my key ring so I can easily access them. It amazes me when I see people buy large amounts of groceries and do not have a frequent buyer card. Even if a person doesn't have a card, they can sign up right there on the spot and begin saving. You can also tell the cashier your phone number if you cannot locate it.

BUYING THE ITEMS THAT ARE AT THEIR LOWEST PRICES

Once you've learned how to identify what is on sale, then you want to see if you have coupons for those sale items. If you are savvy at following the store ads, you can do it yourself. However, if you would like to pay someone to help tell you which items are at their rock bottom that go with the coupons that were just in this week's Sunday paper, then you will want to subscribe to www.thegrocerygame.com.

It frustrates most people when they do all of the coupon work, and find the items shown are way too expensive to even be considered a good deal. The Grocery Game website will show you in green which grocery items are free that week; which items are in blue because they are excellent prices; and, which items are in black – decent prices when used with a coupon but not a steal of a deal. You pay a nominal fee each month to register with this site, then you specify which store you usually shop at, check the items you would like to purchase, and print your own customized list.

REAL SIMPLE partners with Target, a Dayton-Hudson corporation and offers tools that help keep you organized. One of the items that I love that I bought at Target is a REAL SIMPLE pad of grocery lists. I just keep this out on my kitchen desk and check off the items when I run out. Some people like to create their own grocery lists on the computer. They print out a stack of their own customized lists and just add or subtract from it each week.

I try to minimize the number of times I run to the store each week. The more times I go, the more I spend. If I can keep it down to once or twice at the most a week, then I feel like I am doing well.

COUPON APPS

Since everything is becoming more and more paperless, there will probably come a day where paper coupons are no longer. There are plenty of apps available now where you can use those to find in the store savings, without cutting a coupon. I was recently checking out at my local Target. The cashier was telling me how their app called www.cartwheel.target.com, saved people so much money.

This Cartwheel app advertises how you do not need to use paper coupons to maximize the bargains. You add the offers to your own version of Cartwheel. New offers are constantly being added. Then, you simply show the barcode on your smart phone when you check out.

Here are some additional sites you may want to check out for additional coupon savings:

- www.snipsnap.it
- www.shopkick.com
- https://getyowza.com
- www.thecouponapps.com

COSTCO PROS AND CONS:

Pros:

- You can buy in bulk and save.
- Milk, butter, eggs, and cheese are what they call "loss leaders". They will often be priced extra low just to get you to shop there. It's hard to beat Costco's prices on these items.
- If you really do an extensive shopping trip, you do not have to go very often because everything lasts so long.
- They often have samples so it's easier to convince the kids to go along with you, when they are old enough.

Cons:

- You need to have storage space for all of your purchases.
- They do not accept coupons, except their own Costco coupons.
- It's often tempting to buy things in the middle of the store (non-grocery items) that were not on your original list.
- Annual membership fee.

In Southern California, one of my favorite smaller grocery stores is Trader Joe's. This is more of a health food type of a store, with non-hydrogenated food products that are sold there. Here is a pro/con list for this type of a store in your area:

TRADER JOE'S PROS AND CONS

Pros:

- It is a smaller store so it is quicker to walk through and get what you need.
- Fresh flowers are about half of the price of your typical grocery store.
- Lots of easy, healthy, quick meal options.

Cons:

- No coupons accepted.
- It is more geared toward a family of four people or less. It becomes pricey when you are trying to feed a lot of people.
- It is not usually a store that is open 24/7, it is open more like 9:00 am – 9:00 pm.

THE ENTERTAINMENT BOOK

I love to annually purchase the entertainment book for the

Orange County area of California, where I live. The calendar year runs from November 1 through October 31st of the following year. The book costs around $40 new when you buy it right at the beginning of the year. If you wait a few months into the new year, it will begin to be substantially discounted. There have been years where I have bought two of these books for a total of $80. We have a grocery store in our area called, "Ralph's" that is a competitor to Albertson's, Kroger, and Von's. Ralphs always has a $5 a month off coupon for their store, when you spend $75 or more. So, when I buy two books, I am saving already a total of $120.

The Entertainment Book also has a number of great restaurants and offers a variety of savings. The really nice restaurants often provide a free entrée when you purchase another entrée. Sometimes, this can be as high as a $25 savings. You still need to tip based on the original price of the meal, but it's a great way to go on a date for less money.

BOY SCOUT SCOUT-A-RAMA BOOKS

Don't be so quick to rush past the boy scouts in the spring outside your local grocery store, selling the "Scout-a-Rama" coupon books. These offer incredible savings! The books themselves usually cost $10 each. These books include a $10 coupon for our local grocery store, Ralphs, when purchasing $75 or more. There are usually at least ten food items that are completely free. I will usually buy 6-10 of these books a year.

EATING OUT

When I was growing up, it was a real luxury to eat out at a restaurant. In many ways, it still is a real privilege but it has become a lot more affordable in recent years. If you've done a great job sticking to your monthly food budget, then treat yourself to a pizza or a meal out. Portions in America have gotten so huge that you can often split a meal for a lot less.

My girlfriends and I have a favorite restaurant: The Cheesecake Factory. When we meet for lunch, we will often split two salads between the four of us. The meal comes with free unlimited bread. When we order iced tea or soft drinks, they will also refill these at no additional charge. As a result, we are able to eat at a really fun restaurant for $10 or less per person.

My kids have gotten tired of me saying, as long as you still qualify, you need to order from the kids' menu. This way they get a full meal, often with a drink and with a dessert. They're often afraid they will be too hungry when the meal is done, and I tell them I will be happy to order them another meal. Or, if they insist that they want to order from the adult menu, then they get to pay for the meal with their allowance.

Be creative, and you'll be amazed at how much further you can stretch your dollar. When we cut out appetizers, dessert, and drinks, this cuts our bill way down and helps our waistlines too.

Be on the lookout for restaurant coupons, like buy a large pizza on Tuesday and get another large pizza free. This promotion was available in my area for a long time. It was easy to freeze the pizza in two slice portions in foil. The kids could just warm it up as a snack after school.

Check your budget for food, see where you are midway through the month and navigate the rest of the month to see if you can creatively eat out every once and a while. If nothing else, see if your kids or spouse can cook a meal to give you a little bit of a break!

THE CROCK POT CAPER

A great way to stretch your food dollars and maximize your time is to utilize a crock pot. Crock pots cost around $25 - $30 for a good sized one. They can be used on your kitchen counter or take them with you when you are camping w/electrical hookups.

We have a funny story in our family regarding our crock pot. One hot, summer evening, my husband, and sister and her husband were looking forward to going out to dinner. I hurriedly said to my nine year old, "You can go ahead and please clean up and throw everything away," as we were walking out the door. I had just fed the four kids and the three cousins a meal from the crock pot. We left and had a wonderful time at dinner and came home to a kitchen that was pretty well cleaned up.

The next morning, I went out to throw some trash away on the side of our house. To my great surprise, there was my ceramic liner of my crock pot shattered on the ground in front of the garbage cans! We live in a canyon area where there are coyotes and sometimes even mountain lions in the neighborhood. Obviously, SOMEONE had left my crock pot on top of the garbage can and an animal had knocked it off during the night. Whoever it was had not even had the energy to OPEN the garbage can.

"Caroline and Claire (who were 13 and 9) at the time, what in the world happened to my crock pot?" Caroline looked at me and said, "I asked Claire what we were supposed to do and she said to throw everything away. So, I threw everything away!" (Fortunately, the rest of my dishes had survived!) There is never a dull moment with Amelia Bedelia living in our home!

KIDS' ALLOWANCES AND FOOD

A lot of people ask me, "Do you give your kids allowances? If so, how do you do that whole system?" Let me first say, that we have tried a number of things over the years some with success and some without. Where we have landed now is what has worked best for us over the past eight or so years. It's been compiled from a number of various people's ideas, books, radio shows, etc...but I have to say that I like it.

We first took the four kids to the bank to open their own

bank accounts. The program at the bank offered special pretend dollars for every dollar that was invested with them. So, each month when the kids would get their allowances they would get additional pretend dollars to save for prizes that encouraged saving.

The bottom line with our family's finances has been to give away the first 10% of our income. It's not our money, plain and simple. It's God's money. He has entrusted us with the money in our paychecks, so we honor Him by giving our first fruits back to Him. We pay ourselves next by putting 10% into our savings account, retirement account, or 401(k) plan. Then, the remaining 80% is left to pay bills and buy the necessities of life.

How do we determine how much each child receives? We give each child their age multiplied by four. So, let's say my daughter is ten years old. She will receive $40 for a given month. $4 will then be saved in her bank account, and $4 will go towards giving. We've recently started to accumulate the kids' giving money and letting them choose what to donate toward at the end of the year. This helps them to learn the joy of giving and let's them have a say in where the money is going.

The remaining $32 is still a lot for a ten year old. She needs to learn how to manage this money and buy her own birthday presents with it. If a little friend invites her to the movies, she can use that money to pay for it. It also helps when we are in stores because if she wants something, she will need to use her money to purchase it.

I am happy to provide my kids with their lunches in the mornings, but if they decide they want to eat out at school, then they pay with their allowance as well.

We give the kids a separate clothing allowance each fall and supplement it in the spring. Other than those "stipends" the kids need to use their own allowance money, or babysitting money, etc… to fund their clothing purchases.

ETERNITY CHECKPOINTS

So how do we keep an eternal mindset in this topic of groceries, restaurants and allowances? Ultimately, we remember that God is the provider of all of our resources.

We all try to show our kids that when we do or do not have money, that God is our provider. We try to live within our means and budgets to the best of our ability. And, with His strength we go about it all with His joy along the journey!

GROCERY TIPS TO REMEMBER

- Clip your coupons!
- Keep your coupons in a little plastic case in your car.
- Keep track of your finances on Quicken so you can really know what you are spending.
- Check the newspaper flyer(s) that arrive in your mailbox each week.
- Avoid going grocery shopping when you are hungry!
- Set a monthly amount for groceries and eating out. Check it at least by the third week of the month to see how you need to modify your shopping for the last part of the month.
- Have the kids order from the kids' menu.
- Share main dishes with your spouse.
- Have your kids order water at restaurants – it's better for them and it'll cut your bill down by a lot, especially when you have a lot of kids. If you do order a soft drink, you can often ask to have a to-go cup with a lid and they will refill it for you.

Bon Appetit!

ETERNITY ACTION STEPS

1. Make your meal plan for next week, based on the sale flyers you receive in the mail.
   Monday
   Tuesday
   Wednesday
   Thursday
   Friday
   Saturday
   Sunday

2. Cut out any coupons that go with your mealplan.

3. Decide now if your family is going to eat out this week, and where. Do you have any coupons?

4. Determine how much you want to budget for groceries and eating out each month. Begin to review this number each week to see where you are at so that you stay on track with your family's budget.

"So do not worry, saying, "What shall we eat or "What shall we drink?" or "What shall we wear?" For the pagans run after all these things, and your heavenly Father knows that you need them. But seek first his kingdom and his righteousness, and all these things will be given to you as well. Therefore do not worry about tomorrow, for tomorrow will worry about itself. Each day has enough trouble of its own." Matthew 6:31-34

Four

Home Remodeling For Pennies

"Dream no small dreams. They have no power to stir the souls of men." Victor Hugo

This is probably my favorite chapter of all in this book. Why? Because there are so many amazing ways to make your home into the home you've always dreamed of, and it does not have to break your bank.

We have owned houses in Chicago, Salt Lake City, and several here in the southern California area. With the exception of the very first home in Chicago, all of the houses were major fixer uppers. I've decided that it's way better to purchase the home and then maximize my resources to make the home the way I want, rather than purchasing someone's decorated dream.

In searching for bargain homes in these various areas, my husband and I have had all kinds of crazy things happen. We went into one home in the Chicago area and the realtor said, "I'll bet you are looking for the bedroom!"– It might have been because it was nowhere to be seen! Sure enough as he stood on the slanted ground, he pulled open the mirrored door to show us the bedroom. This was the same realtor who was sitting at his desk waiting for clueless people like us to come by in his storefront!

Our home that we live in today we love. However, before we

were able to even see the inside, the seller would only let us see the backyard even though the house was technically on the market. It could be because the inside had concrete slab flooring and plywood on the stairs, or pink and purple walls. There was even a room completely devoted to "I Love Lucy."

Our last realtor, Nora, was amazed at our vision and ability to see beyond the mess. If we wouldn't have had the vision, we wouldn't have the home we have today. As always with four kids, we are kind of forced to maximize what we have to the best of our ability. So, if you are currently looking for a home, keep an open mind, try to not get discouraged or depressed.

Take your magazine photos with you in a binder of what you would like your home to someday look like. Look at the resources you have been entrusted with, and figure out your range of home affordability. And then, pray! Pray that God would lead you to exactly the perfect home for you and your family. Pray against discouragement and the comparison trap.

Once you have purchased or rented your home, choose three main colors to decorate with throughout. It keeps things much more simple and flowing. Here are some tips to remember in the remodel process:

1. Keep the master bedroom/bath the same color as the overall living room/family room color. It flows better this way and is not so choppy.
2. Keep the same tones with your three colors.
3. Go back to your furniture pictures that you love and examine the decorating of the rooms in the background. You might see some paint colors are styles that absolutely grab you.
4. Choose what kind of flooring and feel you would like to have: wood floors which are warmer and more cozy, tile floors which are more low maintenance but can be cold in the wintertime, or carpet which is the quietest but most difficult to

keep clean.

5. Make an overall wish list of what you would love to do with your home, assuming money was no object. Over time you can begin to chip away at this list.
6. If you only have a small amount to work with at first, put it into your main living areas where you will be spending the most time. You can redo the master bath that no one but you sees, some later time.
7. Make any structural changes and counter top changes first. Next do the floors and baseboards, and finally finish by painting last.
8. Don't forget to identify landscaping work you would like to do outside as well and to build this into the budget at some point.
9. Choose a time in your schedule when you have some margin to coordinate a remodel. It will take time and energy.
10. Keep your cell phone on you at all times, and treat that phone as your way of staying connected with the workmen and all of the things you will need to evaluate.

LOOKING FOR THE RIGHT WORKERS

Depending on your budget, you may want to do a lot of the work yourself. This is obviously the cheapest route and will gain you the biggest bang for your buck when you eventually sell your property.

Many times the work is too complicated for the average homeowner and you will need to hire someone to help you out. I highly suggest starting with referrals. Check with your friends who have worked with individuals before. See if their work ethic was strong. Were they on time? Did they deliver as promised? Are they happy to refer them to you? Did they trust them? Are they bonded/insured? Is their license current?

I can't stress how important it is to choose wisely and carefully the people you have working for you. Again, we have seen the gamut of individuals in our experience. We have had incredible individuals and we have had unbelievable experiences.

We had a painter who we had paid for about 90% of the job, and he still had some important work to do in our home, and he never returned. In fact, he left all of his tools at our house. I tried calling him at least two dozen times and could never reach him. The day before he had left, I had paid him up to the 90% point and even had baked him a birthday cake. A friend ran into him years later at a McDonald's. He had sadly fallen back into a lifestyle of drugs and alcohol. He is still one of the best painters I've ever used.

We also had a painter scrape popcorn off one of our house's ceilings. We thought he was a great guy. In fact, he showed us how proud he was of scraping the word JESUS in the ceiling prior to scraping it clean. We later found out that he and his friend were using the time that we were paying them for to take care of their boat in our driveway. They even spent the night in our empty home with their Labrador dog because they did not want to drive back to Manhattan Beach. The lesson we learned from this experience was never pay by the hour, unless you are there to fully supervise!

CHOOSING A GENERAL CONTRACTOR

The aforementioned examples are pertaining to workmen and I just want to make a special note that when you choose a general contractor it is a whole different ballgame. You need to REALLY do your homework. We had a wonderful experience with the contractor who did an addition for us, and have known other people who have had incredible nightmares because of their contractors. Looking back, I think we were incredibly fortunate because I don't believe we understood just how much could potentially go wrong.

Here are some of the major guidelines I would suggest when choosing a contractor:

- Check at least three references from their prior work and check to see that he is currently bonded, licensed, and insured.
- How close to budget was the contractor on prior jobs?
- How close to the completion date were they?
- What was their crew like?
- How will you be billed throughout the project?
- Will you write the checks to the subcontractors or all of the checks to the contractor? (When you write the checks to the subcontractors you at least know what is happening with your money.)
- Does the contractor have an architect that he normally works with? Are the architect's fees reasonable?
- Will you be charged for a port-a-potty on your property or will they use your restroom?
- Does the contractor charge you extra for all of the city permits and fees or does he help you navigate the process at cost?
- How familiar is your contractor with your city's building department? How familiar is he with the city inspector(s)?
- Has your contractor worked with your Homeowner's Association (HOA) before?
- Does he have a pleasant working relationship and understand the necessary steps?

As I have learned, there are many important things to consider when choosing your contractor. So, please choose wisely. This individual will almost feel like a family member for a while because he will be at your house from sunup to sundown. It's very similar to the Tom Hanks' movie, "The Money Pit," believe me!

HOW TO USE CRAIG'S LIST FOR YOUR HOME IMPROVEMENT PROJECTS

Once you've determined the extent of your home renovation project, you will be able to use Craig's List very similar to the way you are able to use it for furniture purchases. Have you had a chance to find any fun furniture deals since reading that chapter? I hope so! I hope you've been able to see how there is so much available right at our fingertips.

First, make your list of necessary items that you will need for your remodel or home renovation. When we moved into our current home, we knew that we were going to add a floor to the open space above the dining room and living room. It is always cheaper to do this than it is to push out a side wall of the house. Our plan was to add a loft over the living room and an office over the dining room. This house had the flat ceilings and not the slanted roof, so it made it more cost effective to go this route.

This dining room had a two foot lower roof than the living room, so that room did involve raising that roof. We debated initially whether we should just put the floor over the living room. However, we are so glad we added the office now as one of the six of us is almost always in that room reading or on the computer. It was one of those things where we had to decide which way we were going to go, as they would build it differently structurally depending on our decision.

Keep in mind, my husband and I have always viewed real estate as a wise way to invest our time and money. And until the recent real estate debacle and falling home prices, it has been a strong investment historically. We have used the guideline: location, location, location, in choosing our homes. This means that where it is located is truly the MOST important part of your home purchasing decision. We have always tried to fix up our home so that it was livable, comfortable, and how we liked it. However, we have never aimed to have the nicest home in an area because we knew we could never recoup the investment.

As we approached the remodel with the contractor in 2008, we knew that there were going to be a number of supplies that were obviously needed. We had negotiated in our contract that we would take care of all of the aesthetics: the paint, the floors, and even the doors and windows. I wanted to do the work to find the cheapest and highest quality workmen out there, and I didn't want to pay my general contractor to do that for me.

With that being said, I made a list of all of the things I would need to buy from a store, Craig's List, or eBay. Here were some of the items on that list:

- New doors and windows for the kitchen, dining room, and loft.
- New hardwood flooring for the downstairs and hallway, loft, and office upstairs.
- Kitchen appliances: double oven, microwave, warming drawer, trash compactor, dishwasher, and range top.
- Knobs for kitchen cabinets.

CASE STUDY: DOORS/WINDOWS

I'm going to share with you how it is possible for you to find these items at a much lower cost than retail. When we were doing our remodel, we actually thought that there were going to be a number of windows from the old section of the house that we could just reuse. However, we found out as we got into the remodel that we had to purchase new windows and outside French doors because the code had changed. As a result, our budget was already maxed and we had to be creative in finding these items.

I searched under Craig's List for windows and doors, under the section household goods and materials/services. Sure enough, there was a man in his 80's who had operated a window/door company in the San Jose area for years. He was going out of business and had carried the best names in the window business. In fact on one of my phone calls with him, he told me how a couple had flown down from Oregon because they were building a brand new house and using all of the windows and doors from his company. This gave me the brainchild idea that my husband could fly to San Jose (a one hour flight), rent a U-Haul, and drive back home the same day.

We had a neighbor who was also in the market for windows and doors so he flew with Carl. As it turned out the products were available, but it sounded totally chaotic and disorganized. You know how men like to go into a store, hunt for the item, and then leave? This involved browsing and looking through hundreds of windows just to find the right size. My contractor had given us the sizes and what we were to look for. However, it just about did my husband in!

The saving grace in the story is that we did end up saving thousands of dollars. In fact, we bought a ten foot high by six foot wide pair of Milgard glass French doors. And basically, we were able to get all of our windows and doors for the price that the one pair of doors would have cost! I think I forgot to mention that everything went well in the transport of the windows and doors as well, until my husband rounded the curve on our street. He went over a speed bump and after nine hours of driving, crash went one of the panes of the windows!! Well, at least it made a better story to tell and we ended up not needing that window anyways!

CASE STUDY: HARDWOOD FLOORING

This is one of my favorite stories from our remodel. I knew I was going to have to devote a significant chunk of our budget to flooring, because there was none. We were working with cement slabs in several parts of the house, so flooring was not an option. However, I was hesitant to purchase this early on in the remodel because I wanted to make sure I had enough money for the essentials. I figured I would wait until almost everything else was completed and then see where my budget left me.

I had worked with an independent flooring man in the past, but he was not able to work within my budget for this project. So, I began searching the internet again. I have a friend who has the Junckers brand of hardwood that is absolutely beautiful. However, I knew it would be out of my price range. So, just on a whim, I started searching on "Junckers". Sure enough there was a posting for enough dark wood to do my entire downstairs.

I called the number on the ad and prayed it was still available. Chris answered the phone and I described my situation. He had had a client purchase this wood and then change her mind. She had paid the restocking fee, but he was now stuck with the product and having to pay for a storage unit for it. He really just wanted to get rid of it at his cost or even less.

I told him that I had an area of square footage upstairs that I needed done in wood as well. I knew I would not be able to afford the Junckers product at full price upstairs. So, I told him that as long as he could use the dark wood on the stairs and match the upstairs in a comparable style and color I would be happy.

He drove an hour to my house the very next day. He showed me my choice(s) and we sealed the deal. He ended up being one of the hardest working individuals in the entire remodel process. He was a man of integrity and did a beautiful job in laying the floor.

The moral of this story is don't give up! Your deal is out

there, it just might take some creative searching. Most of the little mom/pop stores have to charge overhead for their business, so you end up being the one paying the difference. This is why I would rather go straight to the source, the individual who owns his own business and operates mainly by referrals instead.

CASE STUDY: KITCHEN APPLIANCES

Sure enough as with any remodel, one decision leads to another and it is very much like a domino effect. We ended up keeping our kitchen very similar to the original 20 year old layout in the home. We pushed the small eating area out six feet and added a kitchen desk, small pantry, and pool closet that is accessed from the outside, in the three feet we gained in the width.

My goal with the kitchen appliances was to go with the Kitchenaid stainless look. There was one series I liked with the rounded handle. So, thus began my search on Craig's List. About twice a day, I would search household goods for "Kitchenaid Appliances". Eventually, through a variety of private parties I was able to locate all of the Kitchenaid appliances I needed from this series. I want to show you their prices so you can see the retail price difference:

Trash Compactor: Originally $800, Craig's List = $40. (This was taken out of a home by another contractor, because the house was being remodeled. It looked virtually brand new.)

Microwave – Originally $700, brand new on Craig's List = $350.
Fridge – Originally $6000, Craig's List = $800 plus $200 delivery fee.

Dishwasher – Originally $800, Craig's List = $125.

Double Oven – Originally $3000, Craig's List = $800. (This oven had been used by a pastry chef strictly to make little pastries and was also virtually brand new.

Warming Drawer - Originally $800, brand new on Craig's List = $400.

Range top = Originally $1200, brand new on Craig's List = $600.

Total original prices = $12,500.
My cost = $3,275 (basically 75% of retail cost.)

There was a time when money seemed to be flying out the windows into the hands of the kitchen remodelers. Brand new appliances across the board were common for many people. Spending $60,000 on a kitchen remodel was not unheard of. Now that prices have dropped so significantly, I am so thankful that I went as cheaply as possible in this area of appliances. I mean really, how fun is paying thousands of dollars for a new oven?! There are a lot of other places where that money could go.

CASE STUDY: KNOBS FOR KITCHEN CABINETS

One of the final pieces needed in our remodel was knobs for our kitchen cabinets and drawers. If any of you have priced these recently, you will know that they are not inexpensive.

I was at a small appliance store and saw a panel of Swedish Iron knobs and pulls that I loved. They were $10 a knob. Since I had more than 30 that I needed, this was again out of my budget. When I got home, I began searching on eBay for "Swedish Iron Knobs". Wouldn't you know that there they were for approximately $1.79/knob?! I was SO excited.

They were listed as a "Buy it Now" price which means that you do not have to bid for the item. They had plenty in stock, and I was able to place my order just like you would for any other on-line catalog company. They arrived in just a few days and were perfect for my kitchen. They came with screws that were the wrong size, so I just needed to go to my local hardware store to replace those for pennies each.

The other thing that happened with the knobs was I was two knobs short. So, I had to go back on eBay a couple of weeks later when I realized it, hoping they were still available. Sure enough they were still available so I placed my order and my kitchen was complete.

HOME WARRANTIES

There is one more thing I would like to add in this section of the book, and that is the benefit of purchasing a home warranty. Usually when you purchase a home, you receive a one year home warranty for appliances and problems you might have. These warranties usually cost somewhere between $450 and $650, depending on if you have a swimming pool included in the coverage. Every time you file a claim, it costs $55 for someone to come out and service it. Once the year is up, there are many homeowners who do not choose to renew their home warranties.

We have found that we have inevitably saved money as a result of having a home warranty. We have paid $55 when the cost of the repair would have easily been $200 - 300. Homes are always expensive to maintain. By having the home warranty, it has helped us to manage those expenses. We have quickly recouped the annual $600 investment.

You can find home warranties on the web such as Fidelity Home Warranty. It's different than insurance on your home or automobile. This type of a product expects you to file claims, and does not raise your rates as a result.

ETERNITY CHECKPOINTS

Ultimately, our home is in heaven and that is where I want to be storing up my treasures. I want to use my home here for the glory of God: to have kids over with their friends, neighbors, and family and friends from our church. It is His house for as long as we reside here.

"Do not let your hearts be troubled. Trust in God; trust also in me. In my Father's house are many rooms; if it were not so, I would have told you. I am going there to prepare a place for you. And if I go and prepare a place for you, I will come back and take you to be with me that you also may be where I am. You know the way to the place where I am going." John 14:1-4

- Remember to work within your budget.
- Choose your contractor, and workmen wisely.
- Try to obtain and pay for supplies that are in your ability to purchase; avoid paying the middleman.
- Go for quality and reputable brands, as they will usually function best over time.
- Be patient as you go through the remodel process as it usually takes longer than is promised.
- Remember to have an attitude of gratitude that you are able to do the remodel in the first place.

Remember, it's a just a house designed to make wonderful memories for you and those you love. But more than anything else, a house also helps to test your character for eternity!

ACTION STEPS

1. Determine if there is a room or project such as putting up bead board in a room that you would like to tackle.
   Room/Project:________________________.

2. Set your budget for this project.
   $________________________.

3. Decide if you can do this yourself or if you will need to hire someone for the job. If you will hire someone, obtain three names from friends who would highly recommend a certain tradesman.

4. Schedule three times for the workmen to come out and give you bids.

5. Select your tradesman, and set a schedule with a deadline of when you would like the project completed by. Offer an incentive for what he will receive if he finishes early, perhaps an additional $50.

   Get started and accomplish your dream!

The wise woman builds her house, but with her own hands, the foolish one tears hers down." Proverbs 14:1

Five

Let's Make A Deal on that Car For You

"Car designers are just going to have to come up with an automobile that outlasts the payments." Erma Bombeck

Cars. Can't live with them. Can't live without them. Cars are great. They get us to and fro where we need to go. Cars can look great, especially when you live in a climate where there is no snow or salt on the roads to rust the cars. However, if your experience is anything like mine, cars can often be incredible destroyers of one's carefully planned budget.

There have been countless times in my marriage where our budget was looking on track and then....an unexpected car expense. Usually these types of expenses are not $60 they are $600. Unless you intentionally budget for car repairs as a line item on your budget, you will be continually surprised and dismayed.

My husband and I lived in Germany before we had kids. We left our two cars at home in the United States before we ventured to Europe for six months. In many ways, it was the best six months ever. We never had unexpected car repairs. We lost weight as we walked everywhere, including carrying all of our groceries back to our third floor apartment. And, we were able to enjoy the scenery as we took the train everywhere. There is definitely something to be said for public transportation and using our money that would have gone to cars for much more memorable expenses.

CAR DRAMA

Many years later, I was one of the teachers for a weekly women's Bible study at Saddleback Church. I became known as the teacher with infamous car stories. My favorite story to tell was when I was being interviewed by Anne Ortlund. Now if you don't know Anne, she is an elegant, godly woman, who at the time was in her early 80's. She discipled groups of women every year in her condo at Lido Island. I was nervous to meet her because I was a little bit older than the usual woman who joined her group. Anne was intentional and she wanted the women whom she discipled to pass on the information that they learned. The younger the woman, the more years to pass on the wisdom.

Anne arranged to meet me at a lovely restaurant at a hotel by the airport. I drove up in my burgundy van. My husband and I had purchased this van used and to be honest, it had given us nothing but trouble from the day we bought it. I had told my husband that I was having trouble sometimes starting the car and he told me a unique way to get it started. So, Anne and I had lunch. After lunch, Anne discreetly pulled out her lipstick and lip liner and neatly used her compact mirror. I, on the other hand, quickly pulled out my lipstick and put it on while we were talking.

As soon as the lunch was over, I thanked Anne and walked to my car. Sure enough, the car would not start. I looked around and could not see Anne anywhere. I got out of the car in my nice suit, popped the hood, and applied my husband's trick. I took off one of my high heels, and hit the car battery. I got back in, and the car started. I closed the hood, drove home, only to notice later that I had a lovely piece of cilantro wedged in my front teeth. Yes, I was still invited to be a part of the discipleship group but I felt like one of the Beverly Hillbillies.

A DEPRECIATING ASSET

In most cases, cars are a depreciating asset. (Collector cars, of course, can at times be an appreciating asset.) However, in most situations, as soon as you drive the car off of the lot, it is usually worth less than you just paid for it a minute ago. Would you rather put your money into a car or save up for a down payment on a house? Would you rather put your money into a car payment or have several hundred dollars a month to invest or add to your savings account?

Cars are usually a lot more important to the man than to the woman. So, in a marriage cars can often be a point of contention. Women, especially moms with children, desire ease, convenience, safety, and reliability. Men, on the other hand, desire speed, status, and the latest, greatest model on the market. When deciding how much to invest in a car, it's important to be like-minded in this area. Come together to compare what is important to each of you regarding the value of cars in your marriage and how much importance you want to place on them in your budget.

PURCHASING A CAR

Choose the automobile brand wisely. There are expensive brands and they are expensive for a reason. Sometimes, they are expensive because the cars do require very little maintenance. So, although you pay more in the beginning, over time, you actually save money because of the minimal repair bills. There are other luxury brands that have very sophisticated computerized systems and anything that goes wrong will cost you dearly.

Ideally, the best scenario is to pay cash for a car so that you are not spending extra on interest payments. The idea of the millionaire who lives next door is to then drive the car until it dies. I am sure you have heard many stories of the Honda that goes well over 500,000 miles.

When you go to sell your car, convenience dictates to sell it at the dealership. You walk in, see the car you want on the lot, and they nicely take your old car off of your hands, no questions asked. However, the dealer will usually give you less than half of what you would get if you sold the car yourself on Craig's List, for example.

It is difficult to sell the car by yourself because you might sell the car and then be without a car, until you locate the right car. However, even if you have to get a rental car for a few days, you will most likely still come out ahead by selling it on your own. By being patient and selling the car yourself, you will end up with a much bigger down payment to put towards your next car.

When selling by private party, make sure that the party pays you with cash and you go to the bank together to deposit the cash, ensuring it is legitimate. You will need to sign over the title to the individual as well. Just be aware and cautious of the numerous scams that occur on Craig's List and other similar sites.

TO LEASE OR NOT TO LEASE

The benefit of driving a car for a while is that you will own it outright. This means no car payments and the car is yours. However, many people today are choosing the lease option. Leasing can be cost effective, as repairs are usually covered, there is a minimal down payment, and the monthly payments are usually less than when purchasing a car.

It is important to consider the long-term goals of why you are buying the car. Will you be putting a lot of mileage on the car? If so, then be cautious with assuming a lease. There are mileage limits that cannot be exceeded or you will receive hefty charges.

Remember, at the end of the lease, you will not own the car as you would had you purchased a car from the outset.

PURCHASING A CAR FOR CHILDREN

As we all know, when we work for something, we value it a lot more. When a child turns sixteen, usually the "need" for a car is so the mom does not have to carpool and drive the child all kinds of places every week. Therefore, the car should be safe and reliable. The bigger the car, the more kids your child can drive (liability), and the more gas the car will use. Safety is of primary importance. Check Consumer Reports for the vehicles with the highest safety ratings.

We purchased a used Honda Civic for our kids with 90,000 miles on it because we knew it still had hundreds of thousands of miles left on it. We paid $6,000 for it at a dealership. The car has been wonderful, with very low maintenance, and extremely reliable. Several years after purchasing it, one of our kids was driving it and rear-ended a car. This is when we were really glad we had not purchased a brand new car for our kids. The damage came to $5,500. We thought the insurance company would total the car. Instead, they felt that it was still so valuable it was worth fixing it. And, the kids are still driving this car today.

Cars are designed to get us from Point A to Point B and help us to accomplish our overall personal economic goals and not to hinder us. When a child purchases his/her own first automobile, the lower the car payment the better.

THE SCOOTER SOLUTION

Just recently, one of our ways of solving the car dilemma was to purchase a scooter. When I was in college, it was something that some of my sorority sisters had and I always wanted. So, many years later, I finally took the plunge, got my motorcycle license and now have a vintage looking scooter. This scooter gets 75 miles to the gallon with very little maintenance. In fact, when all of the cars are being driven by our kids and myself included, my husband has been known to drive the scooter for over an hour to work! Kind of a fun solution to the pricey car dilemma.

ETERNITY CHECKPOINTS

- Consider how fortunate you are to even be able to own one automobile, or perhaps two or three. Many people in the world walk for miles because they will never be able to own their own vehicle.
- Remember there are no cars in heaven. He who dies with the most toys does not win.
- Your value is in the Lord, not in what type of car you drive.

ETERNITY ACTIONPOINTS

- Calculate your budget for the last twelve months and see how much money you put into your automobile with gasoline, car payments, insurance, repairs, etc...Do you want to be spending this much on your car? Or, are there ways to trim these expenses?
- Do you have an old car that is just sitting on your driveway? If so, there are many car ministries which will accept your car as a tax exempt donation.
- Ask yourself, is your status based in the type of vehicle you drive?
- Finally, when it comes to automobile purchases, ask yourself, what would Jesus do?

"Cast but a glance at riches, and they are gone, for they will surely sprout wings and fly off to the sky like an eagle." Proverbs 23:5

Six

Surprisingly Beautiful Clothes For Your Closet

"The expression a woman wears on her face is far more important than the clothes she wears on her back." Dale Carnegie

I know if you are a woman reading this book, you love to get a bargain on your clothing just like I do. The fun part about clothing bargains is they can be so cheap...a darling blouse for .99. The tempting part is staying within one's budget even when it is a deal that seems impossible to pass by.

First of all, let's address the question of why would a woman want beautiful clothes for her closet? Some women might say for status, because beautiful clothes reflect power and position in society. Some might say in order to wear the latest fashion, and to be hip and with the "in culture" at the time. Ultimately, we are each children of the king and as women, princesses of the King. When we dress ourselves nicely and care about our appearance, we are reflecting Him.

1 Peter 3:3-4 reads, "Your beauty should not come from outward adornment, such as braided hair and the wearing of gold jewelry and fine clothes. Instead, it should be that of your inner self, the unfading beauty of a gentle and quiet spirit, which is of great worth in God's sight."

A woman can be dressed to the nines in a tremendously expensive outfit, of fine fabrics, made by a well known designer, but if there is no beauty inside, it is of no worth.

When a woman fears the Lord and understands that He has fearfully and wonderfully made her, then she can get her eyes off of herself and allow His light to shine through her.

So, in looking for beautiful clothes for a closet...a few things to keep in mind:

- Does it fit within my clothing budget for the month?
- Do I need this item of clothing?
- Do I already have a similar item so I could give the one in my closet away?
- Is it a great price on the item? If I wait a little while, will the price come down?

SELECTING CERTAIN DESIGNERS THAT WORK FOR YOU

Are you maxed out on time? Do you have time to go to the mall to wander the various stores and find an item that fits you? Or, have you found a designer that fits you like a glove and virtually everything you try on was made for you?

I find that the older I get the less time I have to shop and look for clothes, and that is okay with me. I have found a clothes label that works for me. So, I pretty much stick with that designer and I know that the clothes will fit, and wear well and look nice. Now, I am not writing this chapter to promote this designer, but I will tell you my secrets. You see, this designer can be costly, and yet I have found numerous ways to find the clothing at bargain prices.

The clothing line that I like is called CAbi, which stands for Carol Anderson By Invitation. Carol Anderson is a designer who sold to Nordstrom and other department stores. She decided to produce her own line and create her company instead nearly a decade ago. Independent sales representatives show CAbi clothing in the homes for their fall line of clothes and their spring line of clothes. Their line of clothes is made for women from age 20 and up. I love it because it is not made for the teenager. It is designed to flatter a woman at the various stages of her life.

So, how do you obtain designer clothing at a discount? Well, the first way someone can receive CAbi clothing at 50% off is by hosting a party. When you host a party in your home, you will earn a certain number of clothing items that can be at a 50% discount. I have had a lot of fun hosting a couple of parties, bringing the girlfriends over, and then being able to purchase my items at half off.

Several of my friends are CAbi consultants. One is involved in leading missions trips to Thailand and helping girls get out of sex trafficking. She uses her CAbi proceeds to help fund her trips. I love to send friends to her to purchase CAbi, because I know it is for such a good cause.

Once CAbi finishes its fall or its spring season, the consultants usually have a sample sale. Usually three to six consultants gather together and sell all of their samples at 50% off or more. So, this is another way to purchase the items at half off.

CAbi also has outlets across the country. The outlets are always a year behind the clothing lines that are being sold by the consultants. So, I make sure that I get a catalog for every season which is two catalogs per year: fall and spring. I save these catalogs and then use them to reference the items that the outlet has in stock. You can call each outlet and get on their email list. They will have monthly promotions with additional discounts.

A benefit from ordering from outlets outside of your home state is there is sometimes no sales tax. I found a darling jacket at the outlet in Philadelphia. In Pennsylvania, there is no sales tax on clothing. So, I was able to purchase my item(s) there and the savings on sales tax more than paid for the shipping.

Depending on where you live, another place to find your favorite brand of clothing is a consignment store or resale shop. In upscale areas, you are likely to find your favorite designer at a fraction of the cost.

KEEPING THOSE CLOSETS CLEAN

Invest in nice hangers for your closet. Get rid of the plastic dry cleaning bags and the wire hangers. Take the time to make your closet a place where you can easily locate the items, and a place where you enjoy being.

How easy it is for our closets to become full with all kinds of clothes that we never wear anymore. Try and make it a goal every six months to go through your closet and get rid of what you haven't worn in the last year. You will bless someone else by doing this and you will have more room in your closet for other items of clothing.

Kids can learn at a very young age to go through their closets. They can take the items and sell them at a garage sale. Or, you can take them and sell them at a children's resale shop. You won't receive a lot for the clothing. However, when they pay you in store credit they often up the amount you receive so it is a win, win for both.

ETERNITY ACTION STEPS

- Analyze your budget so that you know exactly how much money you are spending on clothing for yourself and other family members every month.
- Evaluate whether or not too much money is going toward clothing in your budget. Or perhaps, it is time to freshen the wardrobe and increase that budget category for a few months.
- Think of the money that you are spending on clothing. Is it a wise use of your money or could you be using that money for far greater eternal purposes?

ETERNITY CHECKPOINTS

- Find someone whom you might bless by giving them clothes you no longer wear.
- Remember that you are a reflection of the King...giving Him glory in everything that you say and do and wear.

"Charm is deceptive and beauty is fleeting, but a woman who fears the Lord is to be praised." Proverbs 31:30

Seven

Traveling With Your Kids for A Lot Less

"Life is either a caring adventure or nothing." Helen Keller

Have you ever heard of the expression, "The world is flat"? Today, more than ever before, the world and our immediate surroundings/competition have gone global. It used to be where the USA felt like one big island. We spoke English and felt like that was all we needed. Why learn another language when everyone else could learn our language? Wow, have times changed. Now, I guarantee you that the person who is bilingual or trilingual has a huge leg up on the person who only speaks English and is applying for a job.

Going global is better for everyone, in my humble opinion. It gives each of us a sense that the world is a much bigger place. It also gives us a better appreciation of other cultures and other ways of doing things. My friend was talking to her granddaughter and telling her to finish eating her dinner. She brought up how there are many children who are starving in the world, so she needed to eat what was put before her. The little three year old replied, "Well, then why don't they move?" Oh, if only life were so simple!

So, if we need to prepare our kids for a global existence, how do we best do that? I think there are numerous ways that are doable and affordable, that will expose our kids to the bigger world that is out there.

DAY TRIPS TO THE INNER CITY OR MEXICO

For those of us who live in California, one of the easiest ways to go to another country is to drive down to Mexico. Just two hours south and you are greeted with another culture, another language, different smells, and an entirely different feel than southern California.

Our church would sponsor day trips down to the orphanage in Tijuana, Mexico. We would sometimes go down there and bring Christmas presents and help the kids celebrate Christmas for the day. It was great for our kids to practice the Spanish they had been learning in school.

If Mexico is too far for you, then do a day trip with your church to the closest inner city. Often times, this too can feel like a foreign culture with different cultures and languages in our very own country.

One time, after coming home from a day in Mexico, our son went to bed talking about how thankful he was that he had a pillow on his bed. Another time when our family was in Chiapas, Mexico, at the far southern border of the country, our daughter watched a woman give her four year old son a pear that she had found in the gutter. My husband didn't even see this happen. However, that fall when our daughter was in eighth grade, she ended up using that example for an essay for her English class.

Sometimes I am a firm believer that travel helps to instill gratitude for the small things. We can talk to our kids until we are blue about being grateful, and sometimes their own experiences speak way louder than our words.

SPRING BREAK TRIPS

Kids like to be needed and valued just as much as we do as adults. We happen to attend Saddleback Valley Community Church, a very large church in south Orange County. They have a lot of options and activities for the kids. One of the things that has worked out really well has been five day service trips over spring break. So, rather than the kids just going somewhere and having fun, they actually go and serve. They took buses to the nearby city of Fullerton (a nice city where I actually grew up.) Hidden in Fullerton was this woman who was a hoarder. The kids completely cleaned her house, her backyard, pulled weeds, and got rid of her stuff. Our other daughter returned saying how great it was to be able to make a difference in someone else's life.

MISSIONS TRIPS

Our church has been fortunate to also offer missions trips to countries all over the globe for the kids to attend. Our eighth grader is right now in the process of raising her support to go to Rwanda in February. We know that it will be too difficult once she reaches high school. So, Saddleback offers a trip for junior high kids to go to Rwanda for ten days. She will need to get Yellow Fever shots and she will need to send out support letters, use any Christmas and birthday money to make it possible.

Does it scare me to send her halfway across the world? Absolutely. Brother Andrew, the author of *God's Smuggler*, once said that "the safest place to be is in the center of God's will." If God is calling her to go to Rwanda, than who are we to stop her? For all I know, she could get hit by a car five minutes from our home. I don't want to be the mom who stops her from doing what God might be asking her to do.

EDUCATION ABROAD TRIPS

Another option for going global is to have our kids live abroad for a semester or a year's experience. Some of the well-advertised programs can be quite expensive. However, there are ways around this problem. Do you know any friends who live abroad? We have had friends offer to our kids to come and live with them and spend a summer with them.

I am fully convinced that the only way a child will become fluent in another language is to live in that environment. They need to be physically present in that foreign country to pick up the colloquial expressions and the proper use of the language. I think it is so unfortunate when kids have taken a language for three to four years and then never actually immerse themselves in a situation where they are forced to use the language.

A book I would highly recommend is called, *The New Global Student* by Maya Frost. This book outlines numerous ways to help engage our children in the world that is around us. In fact, our oldest daughter, Caroline, read this book and it changed her life. The book told us about the Rotary Exchange Program. A child goes to another country for a full school year while in high school and lives with a host family. When Caroline read this book, she had just finished her sophomore year of high school. She decided she really wanted to do this, so she accelerated her junior year and took additional classes so she could graduate early.

She had taken four years of Spanish up until that point, so she requested to be placed in Spain. A year later, we took her to the airport so she could go and live in the little seaside town of Altea. She lived with a wonderful family and became fluent in Spanish. She applied to colleges from Spain, thanks to the internet. Her GPA was calculated based on her California high school. The transcript from Spain was submitted to the colleges as a supplemental record, but it was not calculated with her US GPA.

I actually called one of the colleges before Caroline left for Spain and asked them what they thought about a child finishing in three years of high school. They said that it did not matter to them at all whether a child finished in three or four years. What mattered to them was what did the child do during that time. They wanted to see that the time was productive rather than they were just hanging out somewhere.

Caroline is now a global studies major at the university with a minor in Spanish. I am convinced this would not have happened had we held her back and not let her go to Spain. Spain truly helped her to become the beautiful young woman she is today.

EXCHANGE STUDENTS

So, if you don't want to travel at all and the leave the comfort of your home, another option is to have exchange students live with you. While Caroline lived in Spain, we hosted a boy named Marco, from Italy. He attended our kids' high school and became fully immersed in the American culture. We did not receive remuneration for this, as another family was hosting our daughter. However, lately in Orange County many of the exclusive private high schools are paying people to host their students from overseas.

Since I am basically a stay-at-home mom, I decided that I would go this route as well. I am already in the midst of the high school years with our other kids so why not? Two years ago, "Tina" or Yatong from China moved in with us. This year, for Tina's senior year, we also accepted Olivia from China as well, to live with us for her senior year. Both girls have been a huge blessing to our family. It has been really fun to help them with their English and to watch them become fast friends, and go through the college application process.

Having the girls live with us has given our kids a greater appreciation for what it means to learn a foreign language and to live in a foreign country. My kids have been amazed at their dedication and devotion to their studies.

FAMILY TRIPS OVERSEAS

Almost a decade ago, my husband took the job as CEO of a non-profit ministry which involved a lot of travel. As he was negotiating his package, I asked him to see if he could request that the family travel with him on one trip per year. I had read a book by John Maxwell where John had advocated this idea. John had seen too many Christian leaders traveling all the time, and their kids became bitter. We really wanted our kids to be able to have a sense of what their dad was doing, and to be able to understand what it meant when we said that their dad was going overseas. The organization approved this request and it became life changing for our family.

We were able to bring our kids to places such as China and Chiapas, Mexico where they were able to see firsthand what happens when Christians are persecuted for their faith.

Using Frequent Flyer miles when you or spouse travel frequently is another way to afford overseas travel. Also, Vacation Rentals By Owner (VRBO) is a way to more affordably pay for your lodging in a foreign country. You can also do a house swap where someone lives in your house and you live in theirs for free overseas.

Traveling with kids opens up all kinds of door of opportunity to your families. Kids are able to experience the world firsthand. They will come back home and some of the things they are learning about in their history class, they are able to see with their very own eyes. It is not always easy and there are a lot of logistics involved with getting an entire family overseas, but it is well worth it. You will have so many hilarious memories as a family.

ETERNITY CHECKPOINTS

- Am I trusting God to help provide me and my kids with a bigger view of His world?
- Is there a way I can get involved locally in an "international experience"?
- Ask yourself what you can do to further your child's experience when he/she is taking a foreign language.

ETERNITY ACTIONPOINTS

- Begin putting away money toward your family's first international experience...Step number one...buy passports.
- Pray about a missions trip that your family might be able to go on that would allow your family to serve together overseas, even if it is just for a week.

"Behold the plans I have for you declares the Lord, plans for welfare and not calamity, to give you a future and a hope." Jeremiah 29:11

Eight

College Tuition for the Faint-Hearted

1. Sleep, 2. Good Grades, 3. Social Life..."pick two, welcome to college!" Author Unknown

Depending on how many kids you have, the thought of paying college tuition for even one of your kids can be quite daunting. My encouragement for you is when God provides a sheep, He also provides a pasture. My husband, Carl, met a pastor in Africa. He had six kids and they had no money when it came time to send the kids to college. He reassured and encouraged Carl that somehow, by God's grace and miracles, they were able to put all of their kids through college with no debt.

CERTIFIED FINANCIAL PLANNER

The first step would be to find a Certified Financial Planner (CFP) that you trust and who others can recommend to you. You will need to see if the planner works on a fee based schedule or how he charges for his work. He/She will meet with you and determine your goals for your lifestyle, retirement, and college costs. You will want to have a plan and an advisor that you can bounce things off of when you have major financial decisions you need to make, with the end goal of saving as much as you can for college.

ADVANCED PLACEMENT TESTS

I know a Certified Financial Planner who actually started recommending that the kids take as many Advanced Placement tests as possible because of all of the money it saves for college.

College costs have skyrocketed. When I was in college in the early 80s, total costs for tuition, and room and board, were $4000. Now, for that same education, room and board alone in the dorms is $14,000. The tuition is $13,000. It is not a joke when you read about the middle class squeeze. The problem is that you make too much to qualify for financial aid and not enough to find an extra $30,000 in your budget per year per kid for college.

In order to take an Advanced Placement test, the child usually takes the Advanced Placement course and then pays approximately $90 to take the test in May of the following year. In order to receive credit for that course in college, a child needs to obtain a 3, 4, or 5 on the AP test. You can go on any college's website and they will tell you which scores count at their school and how many credits they are worth. In some colleges, a child needs to get a 4 or a 5 whereas others schools will allow a 3.

We have found for two of our kids that they will basically be eligible to graduate in three years from college, a savings of approximately $60,000.

SCHOLARSHIPS

Another way to help reduce the cost of college is to have your child apply for scholarships. I know one mom who paid her child $20 for every application he completed. Sometimes scholarships can be applied for during one's junior year but most times it occurs during their senior year. Because this year is often so busy and intense for the students, it helps if the mom or dad oversees this process and assists the child in navigating all of the applications.

PRIVATE VS. PUBLIC SCHOOLS

We have done a lot of research regarding schools in California as well as throughout the nation. Basically, you will find that your cheapest route will be the state school in the state in which you reside. Since we live in California, our cheapest route would first be the community college route. This allows a student to get their AA degree in a very affordable manner in two years. You save huge amounts of costs and tuition by going this route. Then, the student transfers to a four year university for their junior and senior years. This basically gives you four years of college for the price of two.

In California, the next cheapest alternative would be a Cal State school such as Cal State Long Beach or Cal Poly San Luis Obispo. These colleges cost approximately a total of $18,000. This is basically a $10,000 savings from the cost of a University of California school (UC) school.

Of course, getting admitted to a school is a big challenge these days. A lot of times your choices are limited by where your child is able to be admitted. It can be a very stressful process. However, at the end of the day, we have really seen that the kids end up where they are supposed to end up and thrive. The key is to not allow your child to get his/her heart set on one school because this can just set them up for disappointment.

The Ivy League schools are about the best bargain out there today. If your child is able to get into those schools, they guarantee that they will meet your need. It helps if your child applies to 8-10 schools. Have them determine the schools that feel impossible to get into. These schools are known as their reach schools. Then, have them choose schools where they think they will be admitted. Finally, choose a few "safe" schools where they should get admitted no matter what.

Tell your child that you will not be able to make a decision until you see the entire financial package that is offered to you.

One of our kids got into a private school in Texas and received an "amazing" scholarship. However, the total cost of attending that school was approximately $57,000. The scholarship took the total out of pocket cost down to $50,000 per year....needless to say, it was not an option.

We saw this frequently where the child would get admitted to an out of state private school, receive an amazing scholarship but the overall cost would still be more than an in-state school.

SPORTS AND FULL RIDES

A final option to consider is having your child receive an offer with a university due to the fact he/she is an amazing athlete. Yes, this still does happen today where the child receives a complete package. However, a caution to be aware of and to remember is that being an athlete at a school is a full-time job. The coach basically owns your child. As a result, the child is often not able to find any extra time to have a part time job and help contribute to college.

It is worth considering using a college recruiting service such as NCSA College Recruiting. You pay an upfront fee and then they set you up with a personalized website for the coaches to view. We used this service and would get a report every day of which coaches viewed our son for soccer.

The key with sports and college is to start early down the recruiting road. A number of kids today commit in their sophomore year of college. So, you don't want to get started during your child's senior year. Freshman year is a great time to start.

CHOOSING TO NOT GO TO COLLEGE

For some kids, college may just not be for them. I have known plenty of kids who are suited to be a cosmetologist, or a hair stylist, or a mechanic. They are not suited for higher education.

Sometimes these professions can actually pay more than those with a college degree.

It helps to know your kids and their strengths and weaknesses and to be able to separate them from your own. I know a number of very wealthy clients who like to use the Johnson O'Connor www.jocrf.org aptitude testing center. They go through a battery of tests with the individual and determine what it is they are best suited to do in life. They will test anyone as long as they are 14 or over. I knew one dad who recently took his daughter to get tested. He had been tested years ago when he was 18. He was retested some 40 years later and his aptitude scores came out identical.

ETERNITY CHECKPOINTS

- Find a CFP and professional tax advisor to best guide you down this road.
- Take your child to visit colleges as early as junior high so that they can see the endpoint.
- Examine how much money you are currently investing in sports with your child and see if it is something he/she would like to pursue in college. This may determine how much you pour into the child's athletic career.

ETERNITY ACTIONPOINTS

- Remember that God is Jehovah Jireh. He is our provider. He is usually not early but He is never late. His glory is revealed by His ability to miraculously provide what seems impossible in human terms.
- Be open to the Lord's guidance in your child's life. Maybe your child is not ready to leave home and needs to attend a community college in order to first mature. Maybe your child would be better suited attending a trade school. Or perhaps your child needs to take a GAP year and travel the world be-

fore going to college.

- Expect and wait on the Lord to provide and He will.

"Now He who supplies seed to the sower and bread for food will also supply and increase your store of seed and will enlarge the harvest of your righteousness. You will be made rich in every way so that you can be generous on every occasion, and through us your generosity will result in thanksgiving to God." Proverbs 13:22

Nine

Living for Eternity with Joy

"I sometimes wonder whether all pleasures are not substitutes for joy."
C.S. *Lewis*

God promises, "*...in me you may have peace. In this world, you will have trouble. But take heart! I have overcome the world!" John 16:33* He doesn't say that we might have trials, He says that we will!

I want to end this book just letting you know that it's okay when you mess up financially. We all do. None of us know the future and as a result, we can make some financially disastrous mistakes. But I need you to know this beyond a shadow of a doubt, God is in sovereign control and He loves you more than you will ever know.

You might have lost money in the stock market. You picked what you thought was a sure thing and then you lost it all. Or perhaps real estate prices were escalating, and you sold at the perfect time. But then you bought at the absolute wrong time because the market crashed right after you closed on your house. You did not know the future, but God did. You even prayed about the decision and you still lost tons of money. It's all God's money. It is not a trite expression to say that the Lord giveth and the Lord takes away, blessed be the name of the Lord.

I love the verse in Acts 17:26, "*From one man he made every nation of men, that they should inhabit the whole earth; and he determined the times for them and the exact places where they should live.*" I love this verse because it makes me know that where we live is not random. When you have your heart set on your dream home and it suddenly falls through, it is not a mistake. God has another dwelling place for you to live. He has different neighbors He wants you to live near.

When you lose everything in a house fire or a flood, He is there with you to help put things back together. It may not be as it was before but it will be good. How we handle adversity is what will make us either better or bitter.

The blogs that I enjoy reading along this same line are, www.lifeingraceblog.com by Edie Wadsworth and www.livingwellspendingless.com by Ruth Soukup. Edie lost everything that she owned in a fire four years ago. She writes about everything being grace, while being appreciative and thankful for all that God has bestowed upon her.

Remember the German proverb, "Choose what you love and love what you choose"? Make your financial decisions with the best wisdom and guidance possible and then let go. Live with no regrets. Pray that God will give you a heart of joy realizing that one day all of the stresses and struggles financially will one day be gone. And yet, how we live today determines the treasures we are storing up for ourselves in heaven. Hold things loosely, realize that it is ALL from Him, and give Him back a portion of everything you receive.

You cannot outgive God. Challenge yourself to be a generous giver, and you will have no regrets. Give God the glory through your life and He will shine and multiply all of the resources He has given you for His Kingdom.

"Now this I say, he who sows sparingly will also reap sparingly, and he who sows bountifully will also reap bountifully. Each one must do just

as he has purposed in his heart, not grudgingly or under compulsion, for God loves a cheerful giver. And God is able to make all grace abound to you, so that always having all sufficiency in everything, you may have an abundance for every good deed." 2 Corinthians 9:6-8

www.ingramcontent.com/pod-product-compliance
Ingram Content Group UK Ltd.
Pitfield, Milton Keynes, MK11 3LW, UK
UKHW020420250726
13967UKWH00007B/2740

9 781467 596312